# The Brazen Horse

Isolde Pullum

# The Brazen Horse

ISBN: 1-933343-30-3

Stabenfeldt, Inc.
457 North Main Street
Danbury, CT 06811
www.pony.us

*For Gaudi, the original Brazen Horse*

# chapter one

I smiled mechanically at the elderly judge as she handed me a beautiful, blue velvet rosette.

"Well done, dear, *lovely* pony," she said in rich, country tones and moved down the line to the next competitor.

"Well done dear, *lovely* pony," I heard her say again.

I patted Basil's neck nervously. If he'd been *my* pony I'd have been thrilled to get second prize at such a big show but I knew his owner, Mrs. Frost, saw anything but first as a failure. It was our own County Show and the day had gone well up to that point. Phantom had won the Novice Pony Championship and Sweep had been first in the Working Hunter. I wondered how her son, Tony, was doing with James in the Riding Horse class; if he could win that his mother might just overlook my performance. I could see Mrs. Frost at the ringside. She was easy to pick out in her elegant, somewhat masculine suit and her neat tray of grooming brushes gripped fiercely in one hand. The winning pony led off and I followed, cantering lightly around the ring to applause from the crowd.

"That was *all* your fault, Paula," Mrs. Frost growled

between her teeth. Her face was smiling expertly, in case a press photographer should happen to be taking candid shots, but her eyes were pure menace. I said nothing. It was useless to answer back.

"You should have let Basil gallop on more, *that's* what lost him first place. Now get him back to the truck before I really lose my temper," she hissed.

I obeyed, glad to get away.

"I hate showing," I told Basil, with feeling, as we walked back to the truck.

It wasn't always like that. When we won she was nice to me, but I was beginning to wonder if it was all worth it. Showing was her whole life and she got so worked up it made her sick sometimes. Her son, Tony, had grown too tall for the delicate show ponies and moved on to horses. Since then she'd had a succession of young girls ride for her, and I was the most recent. The others had left, partly because of Mrs. Frost's unreasonable moods, and partly because Tony was horrible to them and treated them like servants. He was always rude to me too, and I wondered if he was jealous of all time and money his mother spent on the ponies. I'd heard rumors about his father, who had left them, but he and his mother never talked about him when I was around. I'd only done the job for a month and had visited some of the biggest shows in the country, which was exciting, but I was starting to feel the stress of not winning every time and it was becoming less and less enjoyable. Tony was seventeen, tall and thickset and very good looking in a dark, mean sort of way. He had a big, gray horse called James which he rode in Horse Trials as well as showing classes. He didn't always come with us, though, and Mrs. Frost and I got along much better when he wasn't there.

When I got back to the Frost's luxurious horse trailer I untacked Basil. Tony soon joined me and began to fill up hay nets for the journey home. He pushed past me in the narrow corridor and I fell backwards, banging my head on the partition.

"Sorry," he said, in a voice that didn't sound sorry.

I made sure that the ponies were comfortable, and then went and put the teakettle on in the little living area at the front of the trailer. Tony slouched across one of the bench seats and stared at me.

"Make me a coffee."

I made a face at him, "I'm not your servant. You can make your own coffee."

Tony laughed at this, "So, you're in a bad mood because Mom's not very pleased with you? It was pathetic to let Basil get beaten by the Cuthbertson's old nag. Mom will probably get another rider for him now, a better one than you've turned out to be."

"How did James do in the Working Hunter?" I retorted. I already knew he hadn't won it because I'd heard the announcement.

Tony looked uncomfortable and didn't answer. He got up from the bench.

"Well, if you won't make me a coffee, I think I'll pay a visit to the refreshment tent."

He left, pushing past me again, uncomfortably and un-necessarily close. I shouldn't have to put up with this, I told myself. Tony's bullying, and Mrs. Frost blaming me if any of the ponies failed to take top honors. Thankfully, the latter was a rare event. Mrs. Frost had such a wide network of acquaintances in the pony world that there were few judges she didn't know and fewer still who didn't automatically assume that her ponies were bound to be the best.

At first I'd thought it a great honor to be asked to partner the Frost ponies. The invitation had come at a time when I was moping around with nothing to ride. My own mare, Bella, had received a shoulder injury earlier in the spring, when we'd fallen at a bank during the Pony Club Area Horse Trials. She had been lame ever since. The vet had told us to rest her for a whole year and hope for the best.

I say *my* mare, but in fact she really belongs to my big sister, Freya, who is six years older than I. Freya had done very well as a junior eventer and was even talking about becoming a working student in an event yard when she decided to get married. It was right in the middle of her SATs, so you can imagine the fuss it caused at home. She had a massive fight with Dad and stormed out, saying she was going to get married and move as far away from home as it was possible to go. And she did. Her boyfriend, Phil, was a Navy man, and within a month they were married and gone. It was a horrible time at home. Dad refused to go to the wedding, Mom was in tears all the time and I was forever being told to go to my room. This instruction

8

I rarely followed, but instead spent hours and hours in the stable sobbing into Bella's warm and understanding neck. It all blew over in the end. One day we got a phone call from Phil to say that Freya had given birth to a baby boy (Luke, seven pounds ten ounces) and we were one big happy family again. We made the long journey to visit them. Luke became the most loved grandchild imaginable and Dad even grew to like Phil. When they came to visit us, Freya seemed young again and we rode for hours together, schooling, jumping and trail riding. She gave me lessons, which really helped me form a partnership with Bella. It seemed quiet and I always missed Freya when she went home, but at least I had Bella to ride, until her accident, that is.

I finished my tea and stretched out on the bench, luxuriating in the warm sunshine that was filtering in through the little, grimy window. The noise of Basil munching hay was rhythmical and almost hypnotic. I was feeling very tired as I'd been up since five. Quickly and easily, I drifted off to sleep.

"Paula, Paula," Mrs. Frost's harsh voice entered my dreams. "The Cutherbertson's girl's pony has gone lame, which means you and Basil can take her place in the championships. Quickly, clean yourself up while I get him ready. They're waiting for us."

I pulled on my boots and fumbled with my tiepin. To my annoyance it wouldn't go through the material and then broke when I tried to force it.

"Here, child, use this," Mrs. Frost was tense and excited as she unpinned the pin which she always wore on her lapel.

Minutes later I was in the ring and I looked around at the opposition. Basil had a real chance of taking the championship, I decided, as I realized that he had beaten all the other ponies in the ring at previous shows. It was down to me, and this time I would show them that he really could gallop.

"Excellent result, well done Paula," Mrs. Frost was very happy.

She smiled as we posed for a press photographer. The championship sash hung gaily around Basil's neck and the red, white and blue rosette ribbons fluttered in the gentle breeze.

Back at the trailer I hung up my jacket and tie and changed my boots for sneakers. Tony was sulking. His mother had shouted at him for letting James down in the Working Hunter class and told him it was because he spent too much time and money in the refreshment tent.

"Maybe I'd better let Paula ride James next week at the Artsfield show. Now do something useful. I have to go and sign for the trophies."

She bustled away leaving me with a sullen, glaring Tony.

"You'll ride James over my dead body," he snarled at me, "or yours."

I helped Mrs. Frost to load the tack into the side lockers, enjoying her rare and probably short-lived approval.

"Before I forget, can I have my pin back, please Paula?"

"Yes, I'll go and get it," I climbed into the truck where I had left my jacket and tie.

"It's not here," I called, surprised. I searched the floor, trying hard to remember where I'd put it when I took my tie off. Had the pin been there? I thought I could recall pinning it to the tie, but the excitement of winning the championships had made my mind a bit of a blur. Maybe it had fallen off in the ring.

Mrs. Frost stood in the doorway expectantly. I could see her good mood draining almost visibly as she watched me searching.

"I hope you haven't lost it. It was my mother's, and some of those diamonds were quite large," she said anxiously.

Diamonds! I thought they were chips of glass!

Tony leaned over from the cab. He was smiling, obviously enjoying my discomfort.

"Maybe it fell off in the ring. I'll go and ask the secretary if it's been handed in," I stammered, wanting to get away from the mother and the son.

I raced across the sun-hardened grass to the secretary's van and waited while a man in a gray suit signed for a large, silver cup. The news wasn't good and I walked slowly back to the truck, wondering what I was going to say to Mrs. Frost. She was waiting for me, her arms folded sternly over her chest. As I approached she held out her hand. To my immense relief the pin lay sparkling and twinkling in her damp, pink palm.

"Oh, thank goodness, you've found it. Where was it?"

"Don't play the innocent with me, young lady. You know where it was. Tony found it, stuffed in the bottom of your bag." Her eyes had turned almost black with anger. She looked terrifying. Outside, Tony's motorcycle roared into life as he rode away. "You are just a nasty little thief."

"That's not true, I have no idea how it got there," I said, close to tears now.

"You expect me to believe that? You could see it was worth something. I was stupid to think I could trust you with it."

"Maybe Tony put it there." This seemed very likely to me as I remembered the look of hatred on his face when his mother had offered me the ride on James.

Mrs. Frost looked as though she wanted to hit me.

"You've been caught, young lady. You're just a liar and a thief. I thought money was going missing from my purse, and now I know where it went."

"That's not true! Honestly, I'd never steal from you," I said, shocked by what she was saying.

"What can you expect, considering the family you come from? Look what happened to your sister, getting married and leaving school. I should have known you'd be trouble too. I don't want you anywhere near my horses again."

"How dare you?" I wasn't going to have my family put down. "How dare you? You're a horrible, cruel, obsessive old cow. You can keep your precious horses." I ran blindly from the truck, sobbing uncontrollably. I heard her shout something at my retreating back but I didn't stop to listen. In fact I didn't stop running until I reached the ramp of the Pascoe's familiar white and maroon truck and the comfortable, capable arms of Mavis. Freya had once ridden for Mavis and Jack Pascoe and they had always been kind to me.

"What on earth is the matter, Paula? Here, stop crying, it can't be *that* bad."

I buried my head in Mavis's ample chest and sobbed. She smelled of perfume and horses.

"Come inside and I'll put the teakettle on and you can tell me all about it. Jack," Mavis shouted, as she led me up the ramp, "we've got a visitor."

I poured out the whole story to Jack and Mavis who listened carefully and made sympathetic noises in all the right places.

"That Tony Frost needs to be taught a lesson," said Jack, darkly. "You're better off out of that set-up, Paula. I've heard so many stories about those two, about how cruel they can be."

"But what if she tells everyone I steal things?"

"Nobody will listen to her. She's had so many people riding for her and it always ends in tears. Everyone knows what she's like. You stay here, I'll go and get your gear from the Frost's truck and then we'll drop you home later," he said kindly.

"Thank you so much." I sipped sweet tea from a cracked mug. I was feeling better now and was beginning to see the funny side.

"I called her an obsessive old cow," I giggled.

"That sounds about right," said Mavis.

Then I remembered that this effectively put a stop to my riding. I sighed deeply and my lip began to tremble again.

"It isn't fair. Now I don't have a horse to ride at all, and I was hoping that she would let me do some Hunter Trials on Basil during the fall," I moaned.

"Something will turn up," said Jack in a voice that was meant to rally me, "Maybe you could breed from that mare of yours, if you can't ride her any more. Breed yourself something nice to ride on in a few years. Anyway, maybe you wouldn't mind loading my tack into the truck while I go and get your bag. I have a few things I'd like to say to that Gloria Frost while I'm at it."

I packed up the tack and patted Jack's scruffy but talented show-jumpers, Ben and Max. Idly, I wondered what it would be like to have horsy people like Jack and Mavis for parents instead of Dad, who's a dentist and talks about teeth all the time, and Mom, who paints and sometimes forgets to go shopping.

Jack and Mavis dropped me at the end of the lane and I walked up the driveway to our house with my bag slung over my shoulder, along with all the cares of the world. I hardly noticed the warmth of the exquisite summer afternoon, or the damp, peaty smell that came from the large, rambling rhododendron bushes on either side of the path. All I could think of was *no more horses to ride*, and the whole summer to fill with something else. Bella called to me as I passed the gate to her paddock and loped stiffly across to see if I'd brought her any treats. I dug deep in my pocket and found a few dusty, oaty remnants and stood there for ages while she licked my hand.

"I wish you were healthy again," I told her, "We're missing *all* the shows *and* the One Day Events *and* the Pony Club camp. You've got to have a whole year off work and even then no one will say for sure that you'll recover."

She nuzzled my hair and I smoothed her dusty, gray coat that seemed to get whiter and whiter with every shedding.

"You do look sorry for yourself!" A familiar voice startled me from behind.

"Freya! What are *you* doing here?" I turned and hugged my sister. I was so pleased to see her.

She was silent for a moment or two, and then she said, "What would you think if I told you that Luke and I had come back here to live?"

For the first time I noticed the strain on her beautiful face.

"I'd be thrilled, but what about Phil?"

"Phil and I are splitting up," tears were beginning to well in her eyes. "We were too young to know what we wanted when we got married. We've decided to go our separate ways," she sighed. "So here I am, about to build a new life for me and Luke, back with my loving family. That is, if you'll have me!"

"Of course we'll have you. I suppose you'll want the big bedroom back again," I grinned. It was a small price to pay.

What a day! Everything seemed to be changing. It was as if my world had spun suddenly out of control. First the Frosts, then Freya. I hoped that was all the excitement in store for me.

"It'll be great having you here," I told her, "and it will be nicer for Luke to grow up in Cornwall than on some miserable Naval Base."

"I hope you're right. At least I'll have babysitters on tap. Mom's hardly put him down since we arrived. Come and have some dinner. The table's out on the lawn since it's so hot."

"There's bound to be chocolate cake because you're here," I said happily. It was my favorite.

We walked up the driveway together; Freya put her arm through mine and said, "What sort of a day did you have? Did you win all the cups as usual?"

"Not all of them," I laughed, "I'll tell you about it later. One shock is probably enough for this family for the moment."

That night I woke up sweating. I'd been dreaming about the revolting Frosts, only in my dream Mrs. Frost called the police who tried to drag me away in a police car. Every time I shut my eyes I could see Tony's nasty, hardened face laughing at me, so I gave up trying to sleep and went downstairs to make a hot drink. My parents were still up and I heard Bella's name mentioned as I passed the family room door so I paused to listen. Freya was speaking.

"So the vet's concerned that she won't make a full recovery, even after a year off?'

"That's right," said Dad, "Apparently, with a shoulder injury like that arthritis almost always sets in. We have to decide whether we can justify keeping her as a pet. She's not cheap to feed in the winter, and of course Paula's got nothing to ride."

" It would break Paula's heart if she went," said Freya, "She's gotten much more out of her than I ever did. I wonder," Freya paused, "would it would be fair to put her in foal, do you think? At least then she would earn her keep."

"Well, if it's a choice between that and having her destroyed, then I think we should look into it," said Mom.

"Definitely," said Dad.

"Tomorrow then," said Freya, "It will give me something nice to concentrate on."

I scurried back upstairs before I was caught eavesdropping, the hot chocolate and the Frosts forgotten. This time I would dream of foals.

# chapter two

The following Saturday morning Freya and I sat at the kitchen table eating toast and sifting through a pile of stud cards that had been arriving in our mailbox all week. According to Dad, Freya had hardly been off the phone, though how he could tell when he was at the office all the time I don't know. She had spoken to the vet first who had said that breeding from Bella would not make the injury any worse, so with this reassurance Freya had phoned for details of a whole list of likely stallions within a two hundred mile radius of our home.

"What about him, Paula?" Freya held up a picture of a leggy, chestnut horse.

"Hmmm, I'm not crazy about chestnuts," I answered, "How about this one?" I held up a picture of a flashy looking bay.

"Oh, no! Bella could never take a liking to *him*!" Freya retorted, "He's got far too much white on him."

"We want to choose a horse that has competed successfully. It doesn't really matter what he looks like," I said.

"How about this one?" Dad had come into the room

and was nosing through the pile. "It's got a horse called 'False Teeth' in its pedigree. That should suit us!" He laughed to himself. "Good grief!" he exclaimed. He'd obviously noticed the fee, "Never mind false teeth, it should be called *an arm and a leg*! Do they all cost that much?"

We assured him that they did and he went off muttering to find his pipe for a consolatory smoke.

By the end of the morning we'd gotten the list down to three possibles. One we both liked was only an hour's drive away. After lunch we set off for the stud in Freya's battered minivan with Luke strapped into the car seat in the back. He must have been used to Freya's driving because he fell asleep almost immediately. She threw the little car around the narrow lanes and I gripped the sides of my seat until my knuckles turned white. She chattered away, but I felt so sick I hardly answered. It was a tremendous relief when I saw the sign announcing the Penborough Stud and we drove into an attractive, concrete yard lined with stalls. A tall, gray haired man came and greeted us.

"Hello, Mr. Hammond," said Freya, shaking his hand, "I'm Freya Graham. I phoned you this morning. We've come to see King Solomon." This sounded so grand that we all started to laugh.

"Come this way and I'll ask if his Majesty will see you!" Mr. Hammond obviously had a sense of humor. He led us to a large, brick stall and ushered us inside.

"Don't worry, Solly won't hurt you. You couldn't wish

for a better-tempered stallion. You can sit on him if you want to, young man," he told Luke.

Luke hid his face in Freya's coat and pretended to be shy, which he isn't. King Solomon was a truly magnificent horse. His presence was almost awe-inspiring and both Freya and I just looked at him with our mouths slightly open. His mahogany bay coat was hard and as shiny as silk to the touch. He was very handsome.

"He's competed in advanced level horse trials and he's won nearly a thousand dollars show-jumping. At the moment my wife just does a little dressage with him," Mr. Hammond said, proudly.

*Beautiful and talented!* I thought to myself, *Some people get all the luck*. We watched while Solly was tacked up by Mr. Hammond's daughter, Lucy, and ridden in the outdoor ring by Mrs. Hammond. She rode well and showed the horse's paces off beautifully, and then finished by clearing some formidable looking show-jumps.

"Why don't you come up to the house? Lucy will make you a cup of tea and you can discuss terms with my husband," said Mrs. Hammond.

"What would you like to drink?" Lucy asked Luke, who had gotten over his shyness and was holding her hand.

"Milk!" he shouted.

"Please," said Freya.

We all trooped into *the* most wonderfully horsy kitchen, full of tack, rosettes and piles of magazines as well as the more usual kitchen equipment. I was always trying to make our kitchen look like this one, but Mom was resisting. I sat in a large wooden chair with Luke on my lap. He idly played with the zipper on my jacket with one hand, and the other he stuffed deep into his mouth. On the table there were piles of papers that looked like letters, circulars and bills. A photograph of an elegant, bay horse rearing up for the camera caught my eye. Mr. Hammond saw me looking.

"There's a sad story behind that little horse," he said. "Did you read about the EVA scare?"

I nodded; I'd read about it in Young Rider.

"That's the disease that can make mares abort their foals. Well, a friend of mine in Springfield imported a Polish stallion last year. He had him tested at the time but they didn't detect it and now he's infected the whole yard with the virus. Jim's had to close down the stud."

"That's awful," said Freya, "Did he lose many foals?"

"Yes, several of his own mares aborted and some of his client's mares too, but worst of all, he's had to have all his stallions gelded. Apparently, once they have the infection there's always the risk that they'll pass it on to any mare they mate with. It's a real tragedy. It ruined him." Mr. Hammond sighed and passed the photo to Freya.

"He's gorgeous," she stated, "What's happened to the stallions now that they've been gelded?"

"His two favorites will be kept as riding horses for his daughters, but the young one who caused all the trouble is barely schooled. Jim can hardly bear the sight of him, understandably. He's received the insurance money, so I wouldn't be surprised if he ends up having the horse destroyed. Probably do the job himself if his wife would let him! She's kept him from doing it before; apparently she's fond of the animal."

"Is he still infectious?" Freya asked.

"No, once they're gelded they're safe. Most horses get it as youngsters and build up immunity. Why, are you interested? He'd be a good, cheap horse if you were in the market for one."

Freya's faraway expression came back down to earth.

"No, not really." she said, "It's just nice to dream. I've got plenty to keep me busy with Luke."

*She might have*, I thought to myself, *but I don't!*

"How cheap?" I asked Mr. Hammond, my mind switching automatically to my growing bank account.

"I don't know really, meat money, give or take a bit. He's a great horse for that." Mr. Hammond was looking at me with a twinkle in his eye, "He'd do very nicely for you – five years old, about fifteen hands high. He can jump a little, too."

I stared dreamily at the photo and imagined myself on top of this glorious horse. Then I imagined myself at an event, beating Tony Frost into second place and taking a huge silver cup from under his horrible nose.

"I'll ask my Dad, but I can guess what he'll say."

I caught Freya's eye and I could tell she agreed with me. I had about as much chance of persuading Dad to let me buy an unknown horse as I had of flying to the moon!

We finished our tea and Freya arranged to bring Bella to the stud during the following week. I would be at school, worst luck. We drove home, and my head was so full of horses that I hardly noticed Freya's atrocious driving.

I spent the rest of the following week trying to persuade Dad to let me have the Jazzman, which I'd discovered was the lovely name of the Polish horse. I tried several different tactics, including emotional blackmail, along the lines of *how could he stand by and let an innocent horse be put down*? Apparently he could, quite easily. He pointed out, for the hundredth time, that we knew nothing about the suitability of the horse. However, even if it turned out to be the most suitable horse that ever walked the earth he *still* wasn't going to let me waste all my savings on it because I might need the money later on to see me through college. We argued and argued until we got very angry at each other and I was forbidden even to *mention* Jazzman's name in front of Dad. I thought it was grossly unfair, and I told my best friend, Ellan, at school. Ellan, who's small and very slim, has long, brown hair and a pretty, elfin face. She hates being small and says she can't get a boyfriend because they all think she's about ten! She just won't accept that everyone envies her slim figure. She has a bay Welsh pony named Rikki. That day, we were walking from Science, which I like, to French, which I don't, so I was going as slowly as possible.

"It's not that we can't afford it," I told her, "because I've got the money that Grandpa left me. It's just that it wasn't Dad's idea and he's incredibly stubborn and hates me having any fun." This last bit wasn't true, but I was feeling very sorry for myself.

"Maybe you could buy Jazzman secretly," said Ellan, who was always full of plans.

"How can I keep a horse a secret?" I asked her incredulously, "Hide it under my bed?"

"I wouldn't mind looking under your bed. I bet it's where you stash all the things you steal," an unpleasantly familiar voice butted into our conversation. I turned to see Tony Frost and some of his senior class friends sneering at us.

"I *don't* steal things – I bet you put that pin there to make me look bad in front of your mother. I bet you stole money from her purse, too," I stared at him angrily.

"What if I did? You can't prove it and my mom certainly won't believe it was me. She's been telling everyone why she fired you."

"Just ignore him," said Ellan, "He's not worth it."

"Are you missing the ponies, Paula?" Tony asked, "Because they aren't missing you. We've got someone new to ride them, someone who really can ride this time," he turned to his friends and they all burst out laughing.

"And how's that lame old nag of yours? Have you had her shot yet?"

"Bella's fine, thank you, and for your information, far from being an old nag, she's going to have a foal next year."

I was trying to sound dignified and nonchalant but it was very difficult. Tony was very close and had more or less pinned me to the wall of the corridor to keep me from

24

getting away from him. I could smell his stale breath. I turned to go the other way but he grabbed me by the shoulders. His friends were calling and chanting now, spurring him on. I was terrified. I brought my knee up sharply and he doubled up in pain, but he held my arm as I tried to run away.

"You little cow," he groaned and then he twisted my wrist tightly.

His friends were laughing at Tony's discomfort and shouting at me to kick him again.

"Frost!" A very loud bellow echoed through the corridor. Ellan and Mr. Richards ran toward us and Tony let go of my arm. The crowd of boys miraculously melted away and I started to cry.

"Ellan, take Paula to see the nurse and make sure she's all right, please. Frost, come with me." The principal led Tony away, a strangely reduced, less frightening Tony than before.

"He's been suspended," said Hayley, a tall, blonde, glamorous senior girl who we all hated. It was lunchtime and a group of us had been sitting in our favorite spot in the grounds eating our lunches, when Hayley came over to us with the news.

"Apparently Mr. Richards found some contraband in his jacket pocket, including a knife."

This last bit of information chilled me. I'd known that Tony was a bully, but I hadn't thought he was the type to carry a knife.

"You were lucky not to get cut!" said Ellan gleefully, "Then we'd all get into the newspapers and be asked how we felt about it!"

"Oh, *don't*," I said, " It's a good thing that you went and found Mr. Richards when you did. I'd have been sliced ham! I'm a vegetarian too!" I was laughing but not inside.

The incident with Tony had shaken me up thoroughly. I was *very* glad he'd been suspended. At least I wouldn't have to fear him at school. The bell rang and a happy normality settled over the day once more.

# chapter three

Dad was very upset when he heard what had happened. Mr. Richards had phoned him, so when I got home everyone knew about it and was especially nice to me. Even Luke had picked some daisies and put them into a tiny pot for my bedroom windowsill. I thought it might be a good time to ask about Jazzman again. Very patiently, (I hate it when he's patient with me!) Dad tried to explain.

"I know you miss having Bella to ride and I feel very sorry for you," he said, "but we've got to look on the positive side. In a year's time Bella might be sound again and we'd be faced with the decision of which one to sell. You can't expect to ride and look after two horses *and* a foal, and hope to pass your exams."

"What if Bella never gets better?" I asked him, tearful at the thought.

"If that happens then we'll have to think again. We can't just buy a horse to tide you over for a year. That would be very irresponsible. Anyway, do you know how many fillings I have to do to buy a bag of coarse mix?"

*I* didn't but I bet Dad did!

"I've got some money and Freya could help me look after him," I was clutching at straws now. I knew that this was going to be the last conversation we would have about the Jazzman.

"Give me *strength*, Paula!" Dad was beginning to lose his temper, "Freya doesn't know *what* she'll be doing in a year's time. Anyway, she's got more than enough on her plate with Luke. Now I don't want to hear another word about it."

I went to bed early, wondering why I felt so passionate about a horse I'd never even seen. Maybe it was the thought of him being blamed for something he knew nothing about, blamed to the extent that he might lose his life because of it. I began to feel sorry for myself all over again.

Bella returned from the stud three weeks later. I'd missed her terribly. I had been feeling lost each long, light night that she'd been away, when I would normally have been mucking out her stable, grooming her or just spending time in her peaceful, relaxing company. I played with Luke instead, but the games he liked best were repetitive and demanding so I often escaped and wandered around the fields by myself. Our house used to belong to a huge farm, which over the years was split into smaller and smaller lots and sold off to people like us who wanted to keep a few animals. We have three small paddocks and a range of buildings around a cobble stoned yard, including an old piggery, which I grandly call the stables. Cobblestones may *look* nice but they're very hard to keep swept and weeded. At one end there's a shed where we keep hay and straw and several plastic trashcans that contain Bella's food. It had all seemed so still and empty without Bella, and now I listened with great satisfaction to her gentle breathing and the crunch of her teeth on the carrots I'd put in her bucket as a welcome home present. She looked very healthy, though not as well groomed as I'd have liked. I grabbed a body brush and sent the dust flying into a million tiny particles that hung on a beam of late evening sunshine. Freya joined me and started to brush out Bella's thick, tangled tail.

"She was scanned at the stud," Freya told me, "She's definitely in foal, though of course it's early yet so we shouldn't count our chickens."

A shiver of excitement ran through my body. It was almost unbelievable to think that inside Bella were the beginnings of another little horse.

"When will it be born?" I asked.

"Give her a chance! It takes roughly three hundred and forty-five days. She's only had about twenty-something so far! It'll be born around the middle of next June."

"Will she need anything special?" I asked, with vague recollections of stories I'd heard about pregnant women having cravings for weird food, like pickles and ice cream.

"No, nothing but good food and peace and quiet, something she's had a lot of recently," said Freya, "which reminds me, have you had any more trouble from Tony?"

"I haven't seen him, but the rumor going around

school is that he's not going to be allowed back next year. Apparently there've been some complaints about him before."

Tony's dismissal had been a nine-day wonder at school, and there were all sorts of stories flying around, none of which seemed remotely plausible. Personally, I was just relieved that he wasn't around any more. The very thought of him sent shivers down my spine.

The summer vacation was about to begin and I got into a nice routine with Bella that included a gentle walk around the lanes before breakfast. We had a favorite route on our walks that took us through the farmyard and past the farmhouse that had been converted into a Senior Center but still had a large and flourishing duck pond in front of it. I missed riding, but second best was having a pony to look after. I even liked mucking out and I loved going to the yard each morning and seeing Bella's beautiful head looking out over the stable door. Sometimes, mostly if I was a little late, she would call to me as if to hurry me along. It all sounds too good to be true, doesn't it? Well, read on.

One morning, not long after I'd gotten her home from the stud, she wasn't looking out for me when I got to the yard.

"Bella," I called, "wake up, you lazy old nag!" I often talked to her like that. She was the only person who'd put up with it!

There was a strange quality in the air, an eerie silence. I was suddenly very frightened but I didn't know why. I ran to the door and looked over.

"Bella? Bella, what's wrong?"

She was standing in the far corner of the stall with her head so low it almost touched the floor. At first I didn't take it all in, but then I noticed the dark, gaping gashes across her quarters and her belly. Next I saw the heavily bloodstained straw. I staggered back from the door, desperately fighting the urge to faint that was overtaking me. I ran, sobbing and gasping for air, to the house and burst hysterically into a quiet family breakfast.

Dad went to Bella while Freya phoned the vet and then the Police. I hid my head in mom's arms, screaming noiselessly, my breath searing my throat, wishing I were dead. Only Luke, dear little two-year-old Luke, was untouched by the atmosphere.

"More cereal, for Luke," he helped himself from the table. He carried his plate precariously across the kitchen before falling in a heap at Mom's feet. It was the first time he'd gotten his own breakfast, but no one was in the least bit interested. Disappointed and disillusioned, he yelled at the top of his voice, adding his sobbing to mine.

I remember that day as being the worst in my life. Jenny, the vet, drove her car into the yard and I ran to see her. On the back seat lay a humane killer and I became so hysterical that Mom had to drag me inside the house again. She had no words to comfort me but she held me for a long time, transferring some of her considerable strength into my body until at last I grew calm again. I listened for the shot that would end Bella's life, and when it came a pain welled through my body, as if the bullet had entered me. The room spun and I gently spiraled away into welcome blackness and a kind of peace.

"Paula, Paula darling, wake up, it's Dad." I opened my eyes and focused. Slowly the confusion lifted and the pain returned.

"Paula, Bella needs you to go and comfort her," he said.

I stared at him, hardly able to hide my anger.

"She's heavily sedated and Jenny's stitched her wounds," Dad continued, ignoring my glare, "she may pull through yet." He smiled a concerned and gentle smile.

"She's dead, I heard the shot," I said baldly, hating him for humoring me in this way.

"Yes, there was a shot," he said thoughtfully, "but it was probably someone shooting rabbits. I assure you she's not dead, though the state she's in she probably wishes she were. If I ever catch who did that to her..." His voice quavered and I realized for the first time that he was close to tears.

"Frank," Mom soothed, putting her hand on his shoulder.

There is nothing like seeing your Dad cry to thoroughly shake your whole world. Feeling more than a little wobbly I went to the stables. Freya was there. Bella was stretched out on the straw, her whole body quivering and her breathing very deep. Freya was lightly stroking Bella's neck and talking nonsense in gentle, calming tones.

"Freya, will she live?" I asked.

"I really don't know," she answered honestly.

"Who did it to her, do you think?"

"I don't know that either. It's hard, but you must try not to dwell on it. You'll need all your energy to nurse her back to health." Freya pushed her hair from her face and continued, "Whoever did this is sick. He or she probably needs help of some kind. If we don't try *really* hard to put this behind us then they'll have injured us too, and we can't let them get away with that, can we?"

"OK," I said, "I'll try." But it wasn't going to be easy.

During the days that followed Bella's attack I wandered around in a sort of daze. There were lots of things to do for her and I was kept very busy, though I didn't go back to school, as it was almost the end of term. The Police visited us several times, but although they investigated thoroughly and asked lots of questions they were no nearer telling us who did it or why. Except for a neighbor hearing a loud motorcycle in the middle of the night there were no clues at all. When I heard about the motorcycle my mind went immediately to Tony, but only for a few seconds I couldn't really believe he would do anything so evil. The Police told us that other horses had been attacked but no one really understood why. Sometimes, they said, people will read about it in the newspapers and go and try it themselves. The newspapers called us but after speaking to the Police they agreed to report nothing for fear of sparking off a series of copycat attacks in the neighborhood. In fact we were all told to keep the incident closely to ourselves. We found this easy because the very thought of it still sickened us.

For three days Bella lay on her side quietly, accepting nothing to eat or drink. We held up her head and dribbled glucose and water into the side of her mouth, but she coughed and spluttered and probably swallowed little of it. Her eyes were glassy and fixed. Once when I was sitting with her she sat up and began to groan hideously before flopping back on her side again.

They were the longest, loneliest hours I'd ever known. Mom, Dad, Freya and I took turns sitting up with her through each night. We were all beginning to look tired, haggard and disheveled.

On the fourth morning she heaved herself up and went to her water bucket. She drank and drank, gasping and spluttering for breath in her haste, and it seemed like a miracle when she nosed the pile of hay and tried a mouthful. She turned her head and looked curiously toward Freya and me, and we hugged each other and cried with relief.

The vet came to visit her and confirmed that she was at last on the road to recovery.

"She still has a long way to go, but I think we can safely say that she's out of danger," said Jenny.

"What about the foal?" Freya posed the question that I'd been too scared to ask.

"I'm afraid it's very unlikely that she'll carry the foal. At this stage in her pregnancy she has the ability to reabsorb the embryo if she feels conditions aren't right. A trauma or shock can have exactly the same effect."

She smiled at us sympathetically and I thought how sad

her job must be on occasion, having to break bad news to people about their animals. I wanted to cry but I didn't have any tears left in me.

"We are very fortunate to have Bella alive," Jenny went on, "Maybe you can think about putting her in foal again next year."

Maybe, I thought bitterly, and maybe the foal would get attacked too. At that moment the thought of so much potential sadness was too much to bear. The long awaited tears welled in my eyes and I ran from the stables, from the yard and into the road, trying to outrun the pain.

# chapter four

The next morning, at breakfast, the world still looked very bleak. I pushed my spoon around in my bowl of cereal, unable to bring myself to eat any. I could tell that Dad was on the verge of telling me to pull myself together but I didn't care. He and Mom exchanged a look and she nodded at him. They have this way of communicating without words that usually I found irritating. Today I hardly noticed.

Dad spoke, "Paula, honey, Mom and Freya and I were talking last night. We've all been worried about you and we want to help."

I scowled at him, angry at the whole world for what had happened to Bella. Ignoring my bad temper he went on, "As Bella's future seems even more uncertain now we've decided to let you have another horse."

There was a long silence while this bit of information sank in. My family looked at me expectantly but I didn't want to be mollycoddled.

"It would feel as though I was betraying Bella after what happened," I said.

"Freya said you'd say that," said Mom, "but when I

spoke to Jenny about it, she said that another horse's company might make Bella feel more secure. There would be two pairs of eyes to watch for danger."

"But what about my exams?" I was deliberately putting obstacles in the way. Something inside me didn't want to be pacified like a child that's lost its teddy bear.

"I'll help," said Freya, "Luke and I will be around for quite a while."

I remembered the Jazzman, the glorious bay horse who nobody loved or wanted. Dad didn't think he was *suitable* but he *needed* someone to care for him, just like Bella did, that's if he were still alive.

"There *won't* be any good ponies for sale at this time of the year," I said, knowing I was being very ungracious, but I was wallowing in self pity and I couldn't seem to shake myself out of it.

"Well that's where you're wrong, smarty," said Dad, who was beginning to get tired of my sulky behavior, "I phoned Mrs. Harvey last night and arranged for you to go and see a couple of suitable ponies this afternoon."

Mrs. Harvey was the District Commissioner for our local Pony Club and she knew about everything horsy that happened in our neighborhood.

"So, Madam, eat your breakfast, do the dishes and tidy your room. Oh, and can you also try and look a bit more cheerful before I change my mind!"

I obeyed him, meekly for once. A little rush of excitement began to flutter in my stomach as I turned the taps on full at the kitchen sink. I had a plan hatching in my head.

As soon as everyone drifted from the kitchen, I put the dish brush down and dried my hands. Trembling slightly, I phoned the number of the Penborough Stud. Mr. Hammond answered, but to my dismay I realized it was a recorded message on his answering machine. I *hate* talking to those things. I took a deep breath, cleared my throat and listened for the bleep.

"Hello, Mr. Hammond," my voice sounded unusually high, "it's Paula Wilkie speaking. Please could you find out if the Jazzman is still for sale?" I paused, not sure what to say next. "And if he is, can you tell his owners that I want to buy him, but I haven't got much money. I can afford about one thousand dollars. Oh, and don't tell my Dad about this, not yet anyway. Thank you." I heard the tape click and I put the receiver down. My hands had stopped shaking so I went thoughtfully back to my cleaning.

Mr. Hammond had not called back by lunchtime when Freya and I set off to view the two ponies Mrs. Harvey had selected for us. I took forever trying to decide what to wear. I couldn't make my mind up between being very elegant and wearing a riding jacket and cream jodhpurs or being casual and nonchalant in black leggings and a bomber jacket. In the end I compromised and wore my navy jodhpurs, long, rubber boots and a navy sweatshirt. Mrs. Harvey was in the yard to greet us, dressed as always in the same indestructible tweed skirt, a short sleeved, white shirt and tough looking, impeccably clean, lace-up shoes. Her remarkably softly spoken voice didn't go with her outfit.

Mrs. Harvey's yard always had ponies in it. Some were boarders, and some had been her pets for years. She lived and breathed the Pony Club.

"Hello, my dears," she looked at me doubtfully, "You've grown, Paula! You'll be *much* too big for Crispin," she said accusingly; her voice was little more than a whisper.

What did she expect, I thought to myself. People grow!

She opened the door of a stall and inside there was a pretty chestnut mare who came over and investigated our pockets.

"This is Kirsty. She belongs to Janet Simpson. They won the Hopkins Cup last season," we both strained to hear what she was saying.

"She looks great," said Freya, "though she may be a little small for Paula. Can we try her?"

Mrs. Harvey saddled Kirsty and I rode her in the ring. She was a responsive pony to ride but my feet were well below her girth and she felt very narrow. Mrs. Harvey looked gloomily at me as if it were my fault that I'd grown taller.

"I'm afraid Crispin is even smaller," she sighed, "you'll need something around fifteen hands high. There's nothing I can think of for sale at the moment."

"That's all right, Mrs. Harvey," I said, so brightly that Freya gave me a very suspicious look, "I expect something will turn up."

We said our goodbyes and drove home.

"You didn't seem very disappointed when neither of those ponies was suitable," Freya commented.

"Didn't I?" I asked innocently, "Well, you know I'm not crazy about chestnuts."

She left it at that and began talking about getting another car, a sports car with a soft top. Personally, I thought she was dangerous enough with a Minivan, but I didn't say anything.

Every time the phone rang that evening I rushed to answer it. This caused a few raised eyebrows but luckily they put it down to a rare streak of helpful behavior on my part, brought on by the prospect of getting a new horse. The fifth call was from Mr. Hammond, and I answered it in the privacy of the hall.

"Hello, Paula," he said, "I've got your horse for you."

"What!" I yelled. My legs felt like jelly so I sat down on the stairs.

"I was just in time. Jim was about to phone the vet when I called. He says he'll accept a thousand for him and he can deliver him on Monday evening, so can you have the money ready?" Mr. Hammond went on to give me Jim's address and phone number, which I had the presence of mind to write down.

"Good luck with him," Mr. Hammond said, "and call me if you need any help. Bye!"

He put the phone down and I was left sitting on the stairs wondering what on *earth* I'd done. Freya came by.

"Who was that on the phone?" she asked.

"Ellan," I lied. "Freya, will you take me into Redchester tomorrow morning? There's something I want to get."

"Yes, OK. Luke needs some new shoes. I could use a new dress, just in case anyone ever asks me out again, unlikely as that seems right now. I'll tell you what, we can have lunch in the Laughing Pig, my treat."

I thanked her and wondered if she'd feel like treating me when she found out what I'd done behind everyone's back.

That night I dreamed about Bella's attack. It was so horribly real that I woke up, dripping with sweat and trembling. I didn't get back to sleep again until the first reassuring, gray light of day. When I eventually got up and wandered downstairs, Dad had already gone to work and Freya was feeding Bella for me. Luke was with Mom, having his breakfast in the kitchen. Most of it was on the floor or on his face, which I found a bit too much to bear so early in the morning, so I took an apple and a banana from the fruit bowl and went to Bella's stable to eat them. I watched her for a while. She ate slowly and without obvious enjoyment; then leaving most of it, she went to the back of her stall and stood quietly. When I went to stroke her she flinched away from me.

"Don't, Bella," I said, saddened by her behavior, "It wasn't *me* who hurt you." But how could she trust anyone now?

Freya, Luke and I headed off to Redchester. Deep in my pocket was my bankbook that informed me that I had $1,573 and some change, which was the money I'd inherited, plus interest built up over the past couple of

41

years. It was an absolute fortune, and I was always being told not to touch it because it would have to help pay for college one day. At fourteen, that day seemed too far away to worry about, and I told myself that I couldn't be expected to be good *all* the time. Mom and Dad would just have to deal with it. To be honest, I wasn't feeling as brave as I had been and now felt sick, due only in part to Freya's awful driving. She parked the car at the grocers and we arranged to meet in the Laughing Pig at eleven thirty for an early lunch. I helped get Luke out of his car seat and strapped safely into his stroller.

The bank was crowded, full of worried looking people with their checkbooks in their hands. I stood, feeling small and nervous, in the line that led to the most sympathetic-looking cashier. When it was my turn I took a deep breath and asked to withdraw some money.

The young woman smiled and said, "Sure, how much?"

Her eyebrows rose considerably when I told her I needed a thousand dollars.

"I'm afraid you have to request large sums of money like that in advance. This is only a small branch."

My face must have fallen because she smiled and said kindly, "In any case, you *shouldn't* go wandering around carrying that much money. You might get mugged."

I hadn't thought of that. I looked nervously around me to see if anyone was listening to our conversation.

"Would a check do?" she asked, "I can print one out while you wait and it wouldn't be so disastrous if it got stolen."

I thought about this for a few moments and then said, "Maybe, but I'll have to make a phone call."

The cashier was very helpful after that and showed me through to a big office and even brought me a glass of water while I called Jim. I felt very important sitting at the great big desk and I wished that he could have seen me. When I got through he sounded very nice and said of course he would accept a check from me and that he looked forward to seeing me in a few hours. After he'd hung up I finished my water and wondered what it would be like to work in an office with a huge desk with your name on a funny plastic thing. The cashier returned and led me back into the reception area to wait while she printed my check, and before I knew it I was back on the pavement and had twenty-five minutes to kill before I met Freya and Luke at the cafe. I headed toward my favorite shop, Matlins, which sells everything for horses and their riders. There is always a wonderful smell of leather that hits you as soon as the door opens. It's a dimly lit shop, completely stuffed full of saddles, bridles, jackets, jodhpurs, hats, lotions, ointments, brushes and numerous other fascinating items to tempt a horsy person to stop and browse. I made a beeline for the saddles and found one I liked that might fit Jazz (I had decided to call him Jazz, for short). The saddle was made from thick, soft, black leather that gleamed in the low light. I chose a bridle to match and was dreamily sorting through a pile of colored numnahs when I realized the time and I had to run all the way to the cafe. Freya was halfway through her second cup of tea and Luke was sucking banana milkshake noisily through a straw. She'd ordered for us all and showed me his shoes and described a dress she'd liked in great detail. I nodded and pretended to be listening, but my mind was still back in Matlins trying to decide between an elegant white numnah and a practical black one.

On the way home in the car I adopted my usual white knuckled grip and sunk as far down into the seat as I could go. Making the assumption that Freya couldn't actually smack me while she was driving, I waited until we had left the town behind us, before I said, as casually as I could,

"Guess what I've done, Freya? I've bought a horse."

I stared fixedly out of the window and sank a little lower into the seat, waiting for the fireworks. Silence.

Assuming she hadn't heard I repeated my statement. This time my voice sounded particularly high and nervous. Still silence.

I turned toward her, and to my surprise and considerable relief saw that Freya was smirking, trying desperately not to laugh. She caught my eye and burst out laughing, making her driving even more erratic than usual (she had to swerve to avoid an old man on a bike).

"I know! I was wondering when you were going to admit it," she managed to say when she'd calmed down a bit.

"How did you know?" I asked her, very surprised.

"I was listening on the phone in the kitchen!"

"Freya! That's a horrible thing to do," I was shocked and very mad at her.

"No worse than buying forbidden horses behind Dad's

back," she retorted, "Anyway, I was worried. You were acting so strangely I thought it might be that Frost jerk bothering you again. I wouldn't have done it otherwise."

"What do you think Dad's going to say?" Secretly, I was very relieved to have Freya to back me up.

"Well, actually..." she paused.

"You haven't told him, have you?" I could hardly believe it.

"I had to, Paula. You two would have had one heck of a fight tonight if I hadn't. As it was he hit the roof. Mom and I managed to scrape him off it by bedtime, and we've just about convinced him to leave well enough alone. He was still angry this morning when he went to work, so I pity his poor patients."

"The first old lady to complain about her dentures will get it!" I laughed at the thought.

"Do you *really* know what you're taking on?" Freya asked, "I mean, horses that have been used as stallions can be difficult, even after they've been gelded."

"I know. It's just that no one wanted him and he *needed* me. It doesn't feel as though I'm forgetting about Bella if I have him."

The feeling of excitement that had been hovering gently around the pit of my stomach began to flourish. Dad knew about Jazz, Freya was going to help me, and Mom, as always, would be there to pick up the pieces. For the first time since Bella's attack I felt positive. Luke and I sang Baa Baa Black Sheep all the way home.

The trailer that brought Jazz to our yard that evening was huge. We had to unload him in the road outside the house, so it was there that I first saw my handsome new horse as he swaggered jauntily down the ramp, unperturbed by his journey. Jim handed me the scruffy halter rope and gave us his blessing, though he hoped never to set eyes on the horse again. As the trailer pulled away Jazz swung around and almost knocked me over. Freya came to my aid and between the two of us we got him safely installed in the stall next to Bella's. The partition wall between them was high, but they could touch noses. After a squeal from each of them Bella retreated to the back of her stall and her eyes became dull again. We both looked at him critically from the doorway.

"He's got a beautiful head and front, but I don't think much of his temperament. Just look at the way his ears are laid back. Careful!" Freya leaped to my assistance as Jazz lunged across the stable toward me and tried to take a bite out of my shoulder. She caught hold of his head collar and smacked him soundly across his soft nose. Immediately Jazz's expression changed and his ears came forward, making his face pretty once again.

"I don't think he's mean," said Freya, "He's just a bully, testing us because he doesn't know us yet. Don't let him get away with anything, and I bet he'll come around," she advised.

I hoped she was right. Jazz had frightened me with his behavior and I was rapidly beginning to wonder what I had taken on. I grabbed his head collar and scratched behind his ear. At first he flinched away, but then he sighed loudly and began to relax and enjoy the sensation, turning his head to make me scratch him in the right spot. His eyes began to close and his top lip quivered. When I stopped he seemed to take a second or two to realize where he was and I was lulled into a false sense of security. This time I wasn't fast enough when he snapped his teeth at me. His aim was true and he bit me hard on the arm. I smacked him with my good hand and went into supper feeling drained, tired and bruised.

The days were flying past and there was never enough time to do all the things I wanted to do. Bella had to be walked two or three times a day as she couldn't be turned out yet because the flies bothered her wounds. She quickly accepted the presence of Jazz in the next stall but without much enthusiasm. Nothing seemed to interest her for very long. Her wounds were healing well but she wasn't the same mare that she had been.

Jazz was also causing me sleepless nights, though I didn't dare admit as much to Dad or Freya. Every day I rode Jazz, sometimes out for a trail ride with Ellan and sometimes in the schooling area I'd marked out in the paddock, working him over small fences to try to make him supple and balanced. He was very stiff down both sides of his body, and he found a lot of what I asked him to do difficult. Simple things, like going into a canter without bobbing his head up and down, Jazz found almost impossible. When I asked him to do something he didn't want to do he always reared. He was very good at it, and could stay in the air a long time. I thought back to Bella's supple obedience and I almost cried with frustration when, for the tenth time, Jazz leaned heavily on my hands and increased his speed alarmingly around the school. Time and time again I asked him to slow down but he refused to listen. His canter got longer and faster until my arms felt like they were being pulled from their sockets. I was in tears, one morning, when I finally managed to stop him in front of Freya and Luke, watching at the gate.

"It's hopeless," I cried, "I can't ride him. He's just too strong for me. I feel awful, as though I'm pulling his teeth out, but when I relax he barrels off with me."

Freya put one hand on the top of Jazz's neck and the other on his reins. As she massaged his taut muscles she gently tapped the reins downwards until he relaxed and dropped his head. Then keeping his head in the same position, she asked him to move his head from side to side. On Bella when we'd done this exercise she could bring her head around to touch my feet, but Jazz couldn't get within half a yard of my right foot and his left side was even worse. Gently, we encouraged him to try harder before patting him and allowing him to stretch downwards.

"You'll just have to be patient with him, Paula. Do lots of exercises to loosen him up, and take everything very slowly at first. How is his jumping going?"

His jumping! We weren't having much success there either. Jazz could certainly get off the ground and he did so with great enthusiasm and enjoyment, making huge leaps into the air over very small obstacles. I found this exhilarating but somewhat scary, as when I expected to take a one-yard obstacle it felt as though I was jumping two yards! Once or twice his effort was so great I could do nothing but slip my reins and lean back on landing to keep from being catapulted forward. More than once we parted company.

I read all I could about Polish horses and their training methods and pestered the local library to death to try to find more information. I realized what a long way away Poland was and my respect for Jazz grew – after all, the furthest I'd ever been was to Washington, DC on a school trip. I was sick on the bus and I'd hated every minute of it.

Though not experienced, Jazz was as brave as a lion and I soon realized he would go over anything I asked him to. As I got used to his way of jumping it gave me confidence to try bigger and more unusual types of obstacles, including ditches and hedges and water.

He was still inclined to bite, but as we got to know each other he bit me in a more companionable, friendly sort of way, pecking at my clothes and nibbling the ends of my braids. Slowly we began to understand each other. To me he was the most beautiful horse in the world. He retained all the presence and charisma of a stallion, loving to be the center of attention. I couldn't wait to show him off to the rest of the Pony Club so I entered him for the novice class in a One Day Event that was being hosted by our neighboring club, the Eastern Hunt. I had two weeks to practice and as each day passed I regretted entering a little bit more.

# chapter five

The evening before the One Day Event was chaotic. Dad's car was loaded up with everything I could think of that we might need. I remembered to pack the studs, my protective vest, Jazz's boots and some grease for his legs to help him slide over anything he might be unfortunate enough to hit. I had two changes of clothes; tweed jacket and velvet hat for the dressage and show jumping and a polo shirt and helmet for cross-country. I love my cross-country shirt. It's got purple, green, navy and white quarters, all of which, according to Freya, are garish and in bad taste! My tack gleamed from all my efforts with saddle soap and metal polish.

Mom sent me to bed early and minutes after I fell asleep, or so it seemed, the alarm screamed in my ear. It was only just getting light and I wandered down to the stables, eating my toast as I went. I mucked out and fed both horses and then tried to judge what sort of mood Jazz was in. It was hard to tell because he had his head stuck firmly in his feeder and the noises he was making with his breakfast were pretty revolting.

"Don't they teach table manners in Poland?" I asked him, but his reply came in the form of a loud sucking noise, so I grabbed his grooming kit and got to work. I had a busy day ahead of me.

I was due in the dressage arena at ten minutes past nine and at five minutes past I was ready and waiting, feeling more and more sick by the second. Jazz was restless. He knew something exciting was about to happen as soon as he stepped off the ramp of the trailer. He was difficult to tack up as he wouldn't stand still, and it had taken me ages to settle him into a rhythmical trot. I was exhausted when the judge finally signaled for me to enter the arena. The test, which had to be ridden from memory, left my brain momentarily. The competitor before me, a boy of about seventeen, riding a dun horse, wished me luck as he passed.

"Thanks," I said, appreciating the boy's dark brown eyes, "I'm going to need it!"

Jazz seemed to grow another hand in height as he passed up the centerline, and then he ignored me as I asked him to halt and instead he spun around until we faced away from the judge. Biting my lip hard I turned him again and saluted the judge. I growled at Jazz under my breath and dared him to put another foot wrong, and then we set off into a trot, a beautiful, rhythmical trot that seemed to explode underneath me. I hardly dared breathe for fear of giving him the slightest excuse to misbehave. I was as still and as tactful as possible, tentatively asking for each movement, but he bucked when we went into canter and for one horrible moment I thought we were going to leave the arena. Our last halt was square, and at least we were facing the judge this time. We left the arena on a long rein and Jazz jogged and skipped. He hadn't had so much fun in ages! Someone was laughing, and when I turned I was horrified to see Tony Frost standing there with his scuffed leather jacket over his riding clothes.

"Not much competition for me with *that* test," he sneered, "I won't start worrying just yet."

"It's his first competition. I wasn't expecting much," I lied. In fact I'd been expecting a better test than that.

"How's your mare? Still a mess, I imagine?"

I stared at Tony when he said that. How did *he* know about Bella's attack? My mind was working overtime at the awful possibilities. There *was* only one way that Tony could know; surely he didn't hate me that much?

"How do *you* know what happened to her?" My voice was calm, but anger was building up inside me.

"I thought everyone knew. We all saw you fall last spring," he replied, but I thought he looked uncomfortable, as if he'd been caught.

"That isn't what you meant. I thought you were horrible, but I never thought you'd stoop as low as that." I was white with rage and a small crowd of people had gathered around us hoping for a fight.

"You're nuts," he told me, "They'll be sending the men in white coats for you soon." He turned and walked away. leaving me with Jazz.

Ellan came running over and took Jazz's reins from me,

"What did he want?" she asked.

"Oh, the usual nasty remarks," I replied. Had he meant Bella's accident, or had he been referring to the attack? I didn't really believe that Tony was capable of taking a knife to an innocent animal, but somebody had. We walked back to the trailer discussing all the awful things we'd like to do to Tony Frost, none of which I could repeat in polite company!

Ellan, Freya and I walked the cross-country course. Calmly, Freya told me how to ride each jump and advised me on the best routes into each obstacle. Ellan told me how big and terrifying they all looked which convinced me that I would fall off at each one! Charmley is a beautiful place, a country riding academy bordered by mature trees and huge rhododendrons. As well as the novice class that Jazz and I were entered in, there was an open competition for adults. The courses ran alongside each other for most of the way but the open jumps were unbelievably large. Two in particular frightened me: one a big, solid table and the other a very wide fence. Ellan walked along the top rail of the spread, pretending to be the acrobat Blondin, crossing Niagara Falls on a tightrope. By comparison our course looked modest, but far more welcoming, and I knew which ones I would rather jump.

The show jumping course looked fair and I knew that there was nothing to worry Jazz too much. When it was my turn to jump he got very excited and bucked and plunged before I got hold of him and cantered him into the first, a small rustic spread. He gave each fence at least half a yard and it felt as though we were jumping at the Olympics, not a local novice event. The crowd at the ringside gasped audibly and pointed at us, as we made great soaring leaps over the diminutive jumps. I was red in the face and extremely relieved when we finished with a clear round.

"Well, *someone* looked as though they were enjoying themselves, but it certainly wasn't you, Paula!" My dear sister was laughing at me again. One day I'll make her ride him, I thought; see how *she* likes going into orbit!

I patted Jazz's silky neck, "Only the cross-country course to go," I whispered to him.

We ate our lunch sitting on the ramp of the trailer. I had Mom's homemade broccoli quiche, but I was feeling too nervous to appreciate its delicate flavor. Jazz was annoyed because he wasn't given his hay net and he stamped his foot impatiently making the whole trailer shake. For a moment I thought longingly of the Frost's luxury horse trailer and compared it to our sturdy but unglamorous set-up.

I changed into my cross-country clothes and watched, weak and helpless, as Dad, Ellan and Freya got Jazz ready for me. Dad put boots on Jazz's clean, hard limbs, Freya put an extra girth over his saddle and Ellan covered his chest and legs with white grease. I was helped up into the saddle by Dad and told to go and warm up by the start. Beneath me, Jazz felt tense with excitement. Every muscle in his body was taut and he could barely contain himself. It took all my fading strength to keep him between my hands and legs, trotting on a large circle near the start. There were several other competitors warming up. Basil was there, ridden by a nervous looking blonde girl, and I noticed the brown-eyed boy who'd wished me luck and I smiled in his direction. He was very good-looking! He smiled back, nervously. Like me, I imagine his mind was on other things.

"You've got two minutes, number 45," the starter called over to me.

I thought, grimly, that he was probably talking about my life expectancy! The seconds ticked by and I took Jazz into the starting box where he stood doing half rears until the countdown got to one, and then we were off, like an arrow from a longbow, flying toward the first jump.

Jazz made nothing of the fences. He jumped them cleanly and cleverly, and I did little more than hang on and encourage him with my legs for the last couple of paces. Never in my life had I jumped so fast or felt so exhilarated. My fear left me, as with each stride I trusted him more. He made a huge leap over an open ditch and rail and got his stride just right to bounce over the corner. He felt fantastic, and my heart filled with pride in him. It was then that the fun began!

I let him gallop on up the hill, using it as an opportunity for me to get my breath back and for him to settle down. What I didn't bargain for was Jazz seeing the huge ascending spread that was flagged for the seniors. Being an obliging horse he changed tack slightly and galloped toward it. I hadn't any strength left to argue, and before I could really grasp the situation he had seen a good stride. I shut my eyes tight – he obviously didn't want my opinion – and went with him. I waited for the crunch of horse hitting wood, but it didn't come, only the soft thud of two good hooves hitting the baked summer earth. I tried to steady his pace but he wouldn't let me, and I wished with all my heart I were riding Bella. At the next two jumps he chose the senior's route and I just clung to him and offered prayers, promising all kinds of things if only I could get off this wretched horse alive. I knew by this point that we had well and truly eliminated ourselves for jumping the wrong course, but as the trees flashed past me in a blur all I cared about was getting home in one piece. I clung to Jazz and went with him as he took his own line, jumping what he wanted and making his way to the finish. My emotions were strangely mixed, mostly fear but partly a growing admiration and pride in Jazz, who was jumping the huge fences so boldly. He cleared the last, a wide park bench, still full of energy, but he thankfully slowed up when he found himself back in the collecting ring, once more amongst his own kind.

"You were very fast, Paula. I don't think anyone else made such good time." Freya was standing beside me taking hold of Jazz and allowing me to dismount.

I collapsed in a heap on the ground, my legs no longer able to support me. Tears of relief welled up in my eyes but I brushed them aside with a grubby, gloved hand.

"What *are* you doing on the floor, Paula? Get up, before you get stepped on."

"I *can't* get up," I growled, trying to make my legs work, "That horse has drained every last drop of energy out of me and now nothing seems to work."

Freya gave me an odd look and I could tell that she thought I was being dramatic or showing off because Ellan was there.

I made one, last, gargantuan effort, this time managing to stand and hobble back to the sanctity of the trailer.

Freya made a big fuss over Jazz, washing him down and then putting a sweat rug on him and walking him around until she was satisfied he was warm and dry. All the time she talked to him, telling him what a clever boy he'd been. I listened sulkily, thinking that he hadn't been *clever* enough to jump the right course or *clever* enough to stop when I'd asked him to! Ellan gave me a cup of water from her thermos and found me a chocolate bar from the picnic basket. After that I felt a little better. I *had*, after all, survived, and Jazz *had* taken those enormous jumps with tremendous style and ability. Looking back on it I could almost convince myself that I'd enjoyed at least part of the ride. Then I remembered the abject terror of not being in control, of riding a horse that totally ignored my feeble commands. I began to tell Freya about the round and to my surprise, when I got to the *good* bits she didn't laugh but instead gasped in horror as I told her about my wild gallop through the wooded part of the course.

"You must have been terrified," she said sympathetically, "Maybe you ought to try a stronger bit."

"Maybe you ought to sell him before he kills you," said Dad. I hadn't realized he'd been listening.

"Maybe a gag snaffle or a pelham," continued Freya, "that *might* do the trick." She paused, thoughtfully, "Did he really jump that spread?"

I nodded, smiling now at the memory of a shocked course official who had watched the incident with his mouth wide open.

"Yes, he jumped it really well... as far as I could tell with my eyes shut."

Dad groaned to himself, then said brightly, "If he's *that* good you won't have any trouble selling him, Paula. I'll ask around."

Freya, Ellan and I went to look at the results, choosing to ignore Dad, as is sometimes best. Jazz was eliminated, but after his awful dressage score it hardly mattered. To our disgust, Tony Frost won with his mother's beautiful gray gelding, James. I noticed that the boy with nice brown eyes was second; I found out that his name was Adam Bray and I committed this to memory for future reference. All *I* got was a ten-minute lecture from one of the course officials about showing off and jumping fences that weren't in the competition. It seemed easier just to listen than to argue, but when he turned away I made a rude face at his retreating back. It didn't achieve much, but it made me feel better.

We gave Ellan a lift home and sang all the way. I was in a surprisingly good mood, considering. It was probably the relief of not going home in an ambulance! Or maybe I was beginning to realize that Jazz might be something really special, if only I could learn to ride him; if only I could be as good as he. There was one thing I was sure about; at least at our next event things couldn't be any worse!

# chapter six

I walked over to Ellan's house the next day. Jazz was having a day off so we took turns riding Ellan's pony, Rikki, around the paddock.

"It was really fun yesterday. I wish I was good enough to compete," Ellan moaned, as she trotted over to me.

"You are, you just *think* you aren't." I replied, and it was true. The only thing that Ellan and Rikki lacked was confidence. "Do you want me to put some jumps up for you?"

"I suppose so, though he always refuses," said Ellan. Sometimes she lets herself spiral down into doom and gloom.

I put up three little jumps made from oilcans and watched as Rikki rolled his eye wickedly as he trotted sideways into the first. He refused, three times, though he was perfectly capable of jumping it. He was a beautiful pony to look at, a bright bay Welsh with a jaunty air. *What a smart-Alec*, I thought to myself.

"I *knew* he wouldn't do it," Ellan wailed.

"Well, of course he won't if you go into it with that attitude," I retorted, "He enjoys jerking your chain. It's his hobby!"

I tried to imagine what Freya would do if she were here.

"I know, have you got a lunge rein and whip?" It was a silly question. Ellan only had basic tack for Rikki, a bridle and a terrible, hard, flat old saddle that was part of her problem. It was very easy to fall off it, as I knew from experience.

"There's some rope in the garage, and I can tie some string to the end of my schooling whip to make it longer." She was very resourceful.

She ran off, leaving me with Rikki.

"You're a horrible, ungracious pony," I told him sternly, "Ellan buys your food and loves you to bits, and this is how you repay her."

His little pony ears pricked so earnestly that they almost touched.

Ellan returned with the rope, which I tied to Rikki's noseband. I flicked the whip at his back legs to give him the idea that I meant business. He trotted meekly around in a circle a few times while Ellan moved the jumps into his path. Rikki is *not* a stupid pony, and with the threat of the whip behind him he obligingly hopped over each jump. We put them up and again he jumped them cleanly.

"Now *you* get on him," I said to Ellan, "and we'll make him do it again."

With a rider onboard, Rikki temporarily switched back to naughty mode, but I swished my whip at him and we both growled, and then he jumped the oilcans perfectly.

"You see," I told her triumphantly, "you *are* good enough. It's a pity you don't have a better saddle, though. Even the best equestrienne couldn't jump properly in that one. Sticky-bottomed riding pants would help too."

"Well, I can't see Mom affording another saddle, especially now that she's been putting in shorter hours at work," she patted Rikki's neck affectionately, "and she says I've got to outgrow these jodhpurs before I get new ones. At the rate I'm growing I'll get some for my twenty-first birthday! Let's take him in now and have lunch. I'm starving!"

We spent the afternoon playing with Ellan's Mom's digital camcorder. We wanted to make a documentary but we couldn't decide what it should be about until Ellan came up with the idea that I should film her making a cake, like a TV chef. Her Mom was out but she assured me it would be all right.

Two hours, a mountain of flour, six eggs and a pint of milk later, Ellan dramatically whisked her cake from the oven, only to find that we'd got our cups and pints mixed up and the cake was a soggy, lumpy mess. We both started laughing, especially when she dropped the cake pan onto the head of her dog, Licorice. Although Licorice is *not* doggie Mensa material, she is bright enough to realize that when Ellan is cooking, food usually ends up on the floor. She'd been hanging around all afternoon, getting under Ellan's feet, with the hope of something like that happening.

Exit one startled black terrier wearing a spring-form cake pan like a collar, and covering the house with the remains of our sorry looking sponge cake.

Enter Ellan's Mom, home much earlier than expected. We hadn't even *begun* to clean up the kitchen yet.

I won't go into any more details except to say that when I was walking home a few minutes later I remember thinking that Mrs. Parry would probably laugh at the DVD when she saw it later. Providing it was *considerably* later.

Freya was in the yard playing with Luke when I got home. She seemed excited about something and called to me to join her.

"You'll never guess who called you today," was her opening remark.

"Seabiscuit?" I answered, not exactly seriously.

"Close, Peter Edmund!"

My jaw dropped open. She was right, I would *never* have guessed. Peter Edmund was just about the best event rider our county had ever seen. He'd won several of the big three-day events and had a string of quality horses that he rode for his sponsors. He'd become a household name when his horse, Mattie, had won at the American Eventing Championships after recovering from a hairline fracture of the cannon bone just two years before.

"What on *earth* did he want?" I managed to stutter.

"You, you lucky duck! Apparently he was watching yesterday when you were being carted around Charmley on that crazy horse of yours, and he thinks the two of you are promising. He must need glasses if he saw your dressage!"

"Thanks a lot!" I said.

"Apparently he's been given some funding to set up training sessions for talented young riders. There's a three day residential course coming up soon, and he thinks he could help you with Jazz."

"And boy, do I need help!" I said, with great feeling.

"He sounded so nice on the phone. We had a long chat. He says he comes to Redchester frequently because his sister lives there, and he'll try to stop by next week to have a good look at Jazz and maybe give you some advice."

This was too much to take in at once. My head began to buzz with all the possibilities. I was actually going to meet Peter Edmund! I might be going on a training course! But best of all, Peter would be able to show me how to control Jazz. As you can imagine, it was quite a while before I came back down to earth.

True to his word, Peter came over the very next week. He arrived mid morning in a green sports car which he said was his pride and joy. I was in awe of him for the first half hour or so. Anyway, it was difficult to get a word in edge-wise because he and Freya were getting along so well. I looked hard at Peter. He was very tall, well over six feet, I thought, and he had very dark hair, thinning on top and graying at the edges. His features were slightly lopsided, giving him a curiously humorous look, and when he smiled it lit up his whole face. I decided that I liked him.

Peter brought with him a collection of different bits for me to try and we spent the morning with Jazz, trying to gauge which would suit him best. I rode in the paddock while Peter, Freya and Luke looked on. As soon as Jazz swung into his low, active trot Peter's attention was on me. Even Freya at her prettiest and most charming was no competition for a horse with paces as good as Jazz's. I found that he went best in a gag snaffle, and it felt wonderful to be able to shorten and lengthen his stride without a fight.

"You won't be able to use it for dressage, Paula, but it should give you better brakes cross-country," Peter told me.

After a while, Peter called me over and asked to try Jazz himself. I let the stirrups down to the bottom hole and held the offside leather while he got on. Jazz wasn't sure that he liked the extra weight but there was something about Peter's authority that stopped him objecting. I watched, green with envy, at the seemingly effortless way that Peter executed near perfect turns, transitions and halts. Freya constructed a grid of jumps for Peter to try Jazz over, and even when we raised them to around four feet, Jazz still bounded over them easily, making a perfect shape. Peter rode across to us, smiling.

"He's great, Paula. If I were a few inches shorter, I'd make you an offer for this one. As it is I'd be afraid of knocking the poles off with my feet."

I glowed with this compliment to my awkward but beloved horse.

"I can see why you may have been having problems, though. He *is* very strong and a bit of a thug."

Peter dismounted and handed me the reins.

"You get up on him again and we'll see if we can't get your leg on him a bit more. That's what he needs, more leg to push him up into your hands. That way he comes off his forehand, making everything much lighter and more balanced."

*Sounds easy*, I thought to myself, *but I bet it isn't*!

Half an hour later I was dripping with sweat and thoroughly exhausted. My legs felt like jelly and my back was beginning to ache, but my head was full of enthusiasm because for the last five minutes we had suddenly begun to get somewhere. I could have hugged Peter from sheer gratitude but I thought better of it because Freya would only be jealous! Instead I hugged my beautiful horse and gave him half a packet of treats to show him how pleased I was with him. I waved goodbye to Peter as he left our graveled driveway with a flourish in his cute little car, and took a sly, sideways look at Freya to try to gauge her reaction. I was right, there was a sort of soppy, glazed look in her lovely green eyes! *She'll talk of nothing else now*, I thought dismally.

It was eventually agreed that Jazz and I could attend the three-day training session. I say eventually because initially Dad said no. First it was too expensive, then it was too dangerous and then he said he couldn't let his daughter go off for three days with a lot of strangers getting up to goodness knows what, goodness knows where!

I blame Freya for a lot of Dad's strictness with me. I'm

sure if she hadn't run off to get married so young he wouldn't suspect me of half the things he does. In the end, Peter came to the rescue and convinced Dad that it was to be a highly professional, impeccably run affair with separate sleeping arrangements. He said that Mayfields, the estate where the course was to be held, was of great historic interest, so the visit wouldn't just be horses from dawn 'til dusk. He also pointed out that it was a relatively inexpensive way of making Jazz and me into a safer partnership. I think Dad took a shine to Peter and was eager to encourage his friendship with Freya. Peter had taken to stopping by at odd times. He said it was because he was visiting his sister in Redchester, but I don't think this was true because the second time he took Freya out they weren't back until after eleven. I was supposed to be asleep in bed but I heard the car and peeped from behind the curtains, and he actually kissed her goodnight!

The next day a huge bunch of flowers arrived from the florist and Freya was really excited until she read the card and found that they were from one of our more eccentric Uncles who had forgotten her birthday.

# chapter seven

Dad drove me to Mayfields, with Jazz and all his tack in the trailer. I think he wanted to check out the place for himself because he actually took a morning off work — an almost unheard of occurrence. He insisted on being shown my room, which I was to share with a girl called Clare. Thankfully we were the first to arrive so I didn't feel too embarrassed about this show of parental over-protectiveness.

"Dad, tell Freya to make a big fuss over Bella for me." I was missing my gentle gray mare already. I thought how differently I'd be feeling if I was to ride Bella on the course – a lot less nervous!

"Don't worry, we'll all look after her. Have a good time, honey," Dad said as he kissed me goodbye.

He left me, quite reluctantly I thought, in Peter's capable charge, and went back to his patients.

"Take Jazz to the stables and settle him in, Paula. I've got to make a phone call." Peter pointed vaguely in the direction of an imposing archway and then started pressing the buttons on his cell phone, so I did as I was told.

The stables were magnificent. Jazz's hooves echoed eerily on the cobblestones as we went from the cool of the archway into the heat of the sunny, open courtyard that was the center of the stable block. We walked around the edge and I read the cards that were pinned to the heavy mahogany doors. The first said Clare Philips and Magpie, the second, to my knee-trembling delight, said Adam Bray and Custar and the third one we came to said Paula Wilkie and Jazz, so we went in. I was struck by the ancient grandeur of Jazz's stall. The pale blue tiles above the enameled feeder were even fancier than the ones in our bathroom at home. The walls were paneled with rich, dark red wood and the hayrack was decorated with four cast-iron acorns. I don't think Jazz noticed any of this. His head went straight to the rack, which some kind person had filled with sweet smelling hay. I filled his water bucket (plastic and battered, which spoiled the whole effect completely) and went to look around the other stalls.

The next names I came to were Julie Simmons and Foxy, then Melanie Rogers and Pintail and finally Steven Mackie and Freddy. *Two boys and four girls*, I mused to myself. *I wonder what they'll be like.*

I didn't have to wonder for long. During the next hour everyone arrived except for Steven Mackie. Peter called us all together in the yard.

"I hope you've all introduced yourselves by now. I want to get started as soon as possible, so could you all be mounted in the yard at twelve o'clock, please. That gives you time to take your stuff up to your rooms." Peter looked at his notes, "Oh yes, one more thing. Unfortunately Steve Mackie broke his wrist yesterday playing volleyball (dangerous game!) but I've managed to get someone to replace him and he'll be arriving this afternoon. Some of you may know him. His name's Tony, Tony Frost... are you all right, Paula?"

I nodded, dumbly, but at that moment I felt *far* from all right.

"Good. Get moving, then." There was a flurry of activity and I pulled myself together and showed Clare to our room. We were to sleep in the servants quarters that we reached by means of a rickety old staircase that Clare said was about to fall down.

"We slept in our trailers last time I came," Clare told me, "but the owners are away at the moment, so we're allowed in the house."

The two single beds were very high off the ground and spread with starched linen sheets and scratchy gray blankets. I watched Clare as she unpacked. She was about a year older than I and had short blonde hair that was beautifully cut. Her eyes were gray but cheerful and she had lots of freckles and a wide smile. I decided to tell her all about my problems with Mrs. Frost and Tony. I felt as though I needed a friend to share it with.

"Does Peter know what happened?" she asked, when I'd finished.

"I don't think so, or I don't suppose he would have invited him."

"Well, try not to worry. You can stay near Melanie and

me all the time. He wouldn't dare do anything then, I'm sure." Clare was reassuring, though I doubted she was right about Tony. I knew him better, and he'd certainly do whatever he liked, whenever he liked. He didn't seem to have the same scruples as normal people. I wondered whether I should phone Dad, but I knew he'd only make me come home. I weighed up the pros and cons and decided that I wasn't going to let Tony spoil my fun. I decided that I had two ambitions in life. One was to get the better of Jazz and the other was to beat Tony at eventing. To achieve either of these aims I had to stay on the course. I made up my mind to ignore Tony, but I hoped that it wouldn't turn out to be easier said than done.

We waited, mounted in the yard, for Peter to arrive. I was starving. It seemed like years since breakfast, and no one had mentioned lunch. I studied the other riders to take my mind off my stomach. Melanie and her gray mare, Pintail, were impeccably turned out. It never ceases to amaze me how some people can spend all day around horses and not get a speck of dirt on their clothes or a wisp of straw in their hair. Others, like yours truly, only need to look at a stable to smell like one! Adam seemed to have noticed Melanie and was already chatting with her. He looked casual but sophisticated in black suede chaps over his jeans. His horse, Custar, was a leggy Thoroughbred, with a plain head and a kind expression. I liked the way that Adam's short, dark hair curled from under his helmet. *He's got nice broad shoulders, too*, I thought to myself. *Some hope!* I snapped myself out of my dream world. Adam was obviously too interested in Melanie to give me a second glance. Peter arrived and led the way to a large outdoor schooling area set in the corner of a gently sloping meadow and told us to warm up. Jazz was very excited by the other horses and bucked when I asked him to trot. Each time I brought him back to a walk and asked him to trot again, and each time he exploded like a bronco. Peter laughed and called across to me,

"I said *warm* him up, not set him on fire!"

I went crimson with embarrassment and growled dire threats to Jazz that only he could hear. He must have caught the tone in my voice because I could see the white of his eye rolling back as he considered misbehaving again. To my relief he gave a deep sigh and swung into his most stunning trot. The lesson began.

"I can hardly move," groaned Julie, holding her back and pretending to be bent double.

"At least *you* didn't fall off." Adam stood grinning, his sweat stained saddle slung over one arm. "Whoever heard of someone falling off over trotting poles? I feel like such an idiot."

"It wasn't really your fault. Those pheasants dashing out like that scared all the horses, and it was just unfortunate that they tried to fly between Custar's legs!" I laughed at the memory and Adam threw his soggy saddlecloth at me but missed.

"Poor old Custar, he hates doing grid work, not like Jazz. Could I have a ride on him, Paula? He looks great." Adam treated me to one of his best smiles that made my knees go infuriatingly weak. Jazz had been a star that afternoon and my pride in him knew no bounds. The fact that Adam, probably the most experienced rider on the course, wanted to ride him was the cherry on the cake.

"You can warm him up for me before our next session if you want," I said rather wickedly, knowing how awful Jazz could be when fresh. "We'll see how great you think he is then!"

"Great?" said an unpleasantly familiar voice, "Is someone talking about me?" Tony Frost swept into the tack room and introduced himself with all the confidence of a film star. He was an impressive sight in his leather pants and biker's jacket.

"Of course, Paula and I are old friends, aren't we?" He was being unnervingly pleasant to me and I wasn't sure how to reply. Luckily Peter came in with several packets of sandwiches and chocolate chip cookies and a rather red-faced apology for completely forgetting about lunch. We all dived in, but my hands were so filthy the cookies mostly tasted of saddle soap and horse. I was too hungry to care.

Clare and I got the giggles when we were changing for dinner. We wondered if we ought to *dress* for it and go down in long flowing gowns, dripping with jewels. Instead we settled for jeans and fairly clean sweatshirts. The bathroom was ancient and housed a large cast iron bathtub with feet like a tiger. The creaking taps had dribbled the water out between spluttering, scalding coughs and I ended up bathing in three inches of water because the others were banging on the door, imploring me to hurry. Clare and I descended the rickety staircase and followed our noses to the kitchen. We were the last to arrive. Peter was at the stove stirring a black iron pot that reminded me of a witch's cauldron and Adam was draining pasta over the sink.

"Sit down, everyone. I hope you all like spaghetti," Peter passed steaming platefuls of fragrant vegetables.

Melanie and Clare placed themselves strategically on either side of me, but Tony was too busy chatting with Julie to notice. She seemed very enamored.

*You're welcome to him*, I said under my breath, *and good luck*!

"He's very good looking, isn't he?" Julie whispered later, as she passed me the plates to stack in the dishwasher. We girls had been *volunteered* for the job of clearing the kitchen, while the *men* went to check the horses for the night.

"Who is?" I replied, hoping she didn't mean Adam.

"Tony. He's got beautiful eyes." Her own bespectacled eyes looked faraway and dreamy.

"I suppose so, if you like rattlesnakes."

Julie looked offended but I didn't care. Melanie tactfully changed the subject.

"Apparently we've got a Captain Hewit teaching us to-morrow. Does anyone know him?"

"Yes, I do," said Clare, "My sister used to have lessons with him. He's very strict. He's got a big moustache and a cane which he points at people he's about to tear to pieces."

"He sounds charming. Jazz is bound make me look bad. He's got a warped sense of humor."

"It serves you right for being rash and buying crazy Polish horses behind your parents' backs," said Clare, laughing at me.

Peter, Adam and Tony came in from the stables and Melanie made hot chocolate for us all, which we took up to bed. As I walked up the stairs, Tony was behind me and he put his hand casually across my shoulder, almost making me drop my cup.

"I like your new horse," he said quietly, so that only I could hear, "Very classy. I see I'll have to watch out in the future."

Before I could stop him he planted a kiss on my cheek. How dare he? Anger swept through my body and I pulled away from him violently. Tony pretending to be nice was even worse than Tony being horrible.

"Good night, Paula, sleep well," he said loudly, so everyone could hear. He was smiling at my discomfort.

Julie glared at me and turned to go to her room without a word. Even Adam looked curious and my heart sank as I realized that he was sharing a room with Tony. Goodness only knew what lies Tony would tell him about me before they went to sleep that night.

# chapter eight

Peter woke us at six o'clock with a cup of tea, which is a better wake-up service than I ever get at home. I sat up in bed, sipping the hot liquid and wondering what the day had in store.

"What's Magpie like at cross country?" I asked Clare who had stopped snoring so I guessed she was awake.

"Oh, he's very good. He's better at it than I am. My sister used to do a lot before she outgrew him."

"Sounds a little like my mare, Bella," I told her, and for a few seconds I felt sad, wondering if I would ever be able to ride her again. I had grown to love Jazz, but I often longed for Bella's calm, capable nature; she was always so dependable and trustworthy.

"Come on, stop daydreaming. It's going to be fun today," said Clare, smiling kindly at me, and I wondered if she sensed my sadness.

Everyone except Tony mucked out before breakfast. Peter fed James because he was banging his door impatiently, furious at not having his food like the rest of the horses.

"Adam, go and drag Tony out of bed," said Peter, and there was a note of irritation in his voice.

"He was dead to the world when I left him. I did try to wake him." Adam put his broom down and went toward the house.

"Oh, leave him," said Julie, "I'll muck out James, I don't mind."

We all looked at her as if she were crazy and went and had breakfast, leaving her to it.

Tony was up in time for the lesson. We were ushered down to the indoor ring by the extraordinarily fast-walking Captain Hewit, who did indeed carry a cane. Our horses had to jog to keep up with him.

"Right, get on with it. Warm your horses up," he demanded.

He leaned on the stick with his arms crossed, looking at us fiercely over his bristling moustache. We had only been there for two minutes when we heard him bellow across the school.

"You girl, with the braid."

He had jumped up and was pointing it at me. Blushing crimson I turned Jazz to face him.

"Yes, you. *What* is the matter? You're riding that horse as if you think he's about to explode."

*Too true!* I thought to myself.

"If you don't allow him to stretch his back, his hind legs can't come under him. You *must* use *your* legs more to encourage him to drop his head – then you can take up the contact. Ride him, girl, don't be scared of him."

76

I nodded. It was good advice, but I knew what Jazz was capable of when he was fresh. The Captain was staring at me as though he thought I was simple.

"Well, go on, then," he bellowed.

I decided I was more scared of the Captain than I was of Jazz, so I did as I was told. At first Jazz responded well to my increased leg pressure and his head dropped enough for his back to stretch. We managed half a lap around the ring in this way before he realized that I had let up on him a little. Then, with a squeal and a huge and joyous leap he sprung into one of his biggest bucks. I was tipped onto his neck, and when he bucked again I flew through the air and landed on the dusty floor of the school with my mouth wide open. I wasn't hurt, but the floor tasted disgusting and I tried not to think of all the horse droppings that had previously landed just where I had! I could hear Tony laughing.

"*No, no, no!*" screamed the Captain, "Not like that! It's entirely your own fault."

Somehow I thought it might be.

"Get up, girl. We'll start again."

I desperately wanted to spit, but something in the Captain's glare told me that he wouldn't appreciate it. Adam had kindly caught Jazz for me, so I gritted my teeth, swallowed and mounted again.

For the next ten minutes the captain concentrated solely on me. He made me sit more firmly and use my legs more than I'd thought was possible. He encouraged me to sit up and ride Jazz through his bucks when they came and to immediately reprimand him. To my delight Jazz began to respond.

"Well done, Paula," said the Captain. We were on first name terms now! "That was well ridden at times. None of you realize how hard you have to work if you want your horses to go really well," he addressed the whole class. "That's especially true if your horse has anything resembling a brain between his ears, and believe me, they are the worst!"

Clare was the next one to get it. We were all asked to lengthen our horse's stride down the long side of the school but Clare's efforts didn't meet with our tormentor's approval.

"That pony is *brilliant*," he said of the smart little piebald cob, "but *you* don't deserve him. All you need to do is half halt to make him listen and get his hocks under him, then quietly ask for a little bit more. You throw your reins at him and kick like mad and *still* he does what you ask, but oh, it looks so inelegant!"

He made us all do it several more times before he was satisfied. We worked on our canter next, then transitions from walk to trot, and finally our halts. To my delight Tony was told off for using his hands too harshly.

"Any questions?" No one dared say a word.

"Okay then, go and feed your horses, have lunch and be back in the yard dressed for cross-country practice by two o'clock. I'm having lunch in town."

He got into his classic red sports car and drove away.

"Thank goodness he's gone," said Julie, "I couldn't have stood much more of his bullying."

"He does know his stuff, though," said Clare.

"That doesn't give him the right to be rude to us," said Melanie.

"If Hewit's going to town, I'd better make sure I avoid him," said Tony, "Look after James for me, Julie."

He handed her the reins and sauntered off in the direction of his motorcycle. To my surprise, Julie meekly obeyed. She was actually smiling to herself as she led James and Foxy back to the stables.

Tony didn't arrive back for the afternoon session, to my relief. He had been keeping himself pretty much to himself but I still found his company unsettling. Captain Hewit seemed to have had a very agreeable lunch and returned in a vastly improved mood.

The cross-country practice was excellent and everyone enjoyed it, especially the horses. The setting in the park was just about perfect. Mature trees, heavy with summer leaves, cast cool and welcome shadows that contrasted with the hot, still day. We wore T-shirts under our protective vests, except for Adam who wasn't wearing anything under his. We began with a three-minute trot followed by a thirty second rest and a three-minute canter. The Captain leaned on his stick and timed us with a stopwatch. Three minutes is a surprisingly long time when you are cantering on a strong, fit horse with your stirrups four holes shorter than usual. We rested for a whole minute and then repeated the exercise. The second canter was much easier – Jazz felt as though he could go on forever and was hardly blowing at all. I was red in the face, gasping for air and I could feel sweat begin to dribble down my back. The Captain called us together.

"We will work on corners today," he announced, "but first you can take them over the logs in this field so I can see how you ride your fences. Julie, will you lead off, please?"

The Captain pointed to a line of six small logs dotted around the field. At my request Jazz cantered behind the others, taking the jumps in his stride as each one came toward us. It was heavenly. He felt so powerful and fit and he was enjoying himself as much as I was. From my place at the back of the line I could see how the others were faring. Julie had her bay, Foxy, well under control but both Melanie and Adam were fighting with their mounts to stay in line. Dear little Magpie was galloping steadily, doing his job well.

We went around twice and the Captain shouted, "Very good, everyone, you're obviously cross-country specialists." He *must* have had a very good lunch. "Go again, but this time really ride them on as soon as you land. Get into a stride and stick to it."

It was surprising how much quicker it felt, though we weren't actually going any faster.

We moved on to the next field, which had a corner or *V* fence in it that consisted of two heavy rails, open at one end and closed at the other. Captain Hewit briefed us. He was like a walking textbook!

"You can jump this in two ways, either the wide bit as two jumps or the narrow bit as one. The pointed bit looks more formidable but is, in fact, simpler, if you have an honest horse who isn't going to run away with you. It's bigger but less tiring than jumping two elements."

I laughed to myself, and then said out loud that most things *would* be less tiring than jumping two elephants! The Captain just glared at me then carried on.

"You must choose your line carefully. I think it best to jump at right angles to the back pole, but some draw an imaginary line between the two and jump at right angles to that. Whatever else you do, you must *never* jump at right angles to the front pole because then the jump gets wider as you cross it. This is unfair to the horse and potentially very dangerous. Any questions?" he didn't wait for a reply, "No? Good! Adam lead on, and the rest of you follow at least ten strides apart."

I was third in line and Jazz began to bounce on the spot, impatient to jump. The corner looked big and solid as I approached it and Jazz was getting stronger in my hands. With my heart in my mouth I lined him up and he had the sense to look for his own stride and carry me over. We did this twice more for each and then went on to tackle the double route.

"The distance between the two elements is less than one stride, so your horses will have to land and immediately take off again. It's called a bounce stride," the Captain told us. "You must therefore approach this fence on a short, bouncy stride to enable the horse to jump off his hocks. This will also give him the chance to see what is going on. Got it? Paula, you first."

Obediently, Jazz and I set off toward the jump. I realized we were going too fast so I sat up and collected him a little, effectively shortening his stride.

*Light and bouncy*, I said to myself. The jump came to us, and we met the first rail perfectly which meant that the second followed sweetly on. Jazz powered over it effortlessly. When everyone else had jumped the bounce to the Captain's liking he told us to string all the fences together. We set off, one at a time, and galloped around the improvised course. Adam sped past me letting out a yell of high spirits and punching his fist high in the air. The sun was blinding but glorious as our horses raced around the fields, urged on by our rush of madness. It was fantastic! Well worth the lecture that the Captain gave us later about losing control of our horses!

That evening Peter took us bowling at a local country club – as if we needed any more exercise after the day we'd had! Clare and I spent a long time deciding what to wear.

"If you're not wearing your gray shirt, can I borrow it?" she asked me.

"OK. Will you do my hair in a French braid?" I asked, "I can never get it neat enough myself."

I put on my new, green denim jeans with a plain black sweatshirt. I was a bit too warm. Clare offered to lend me her white T-shirt, but I knew my chest was too big to look nice in it.

82

"You're lucky," I said, looking at her neat, flattish torso.

"You *are* joking," she laughed, "I'd kill to have yours!"

"Not if you had it you wouldn't," I moaned. " People always think I'm older than I am. Boys *look*, too!" I started to laugh at myself, it all sounded so pathetic.

"Well I don't consider that much of a problem," Clare looked genuinely surprised, "It's when boys don't look that you've got to worry!"

Clare braided my hair beautifully, finishing off the end with a black bow. She flicked a comb expertly through her own short blonde hair that was cut to the line of her jawbone.

"I wish I had pierced ears," I looked enviously at Clare's pretty gold hoops, "but my Dad absolutely forbids it!"

We went and waited in the hall. I was hopeful that Adam might take some notice of me until I saw Melanie. She was wearing designer jeans, which I knew must have cost a small fortune, a real silk blouse and tons of make-up. She looked about eighteen and I felt about twelve by comparison! I sighed. What was the point of trying to compete with her natural good looks and apparently boundless clothes allowance? She seemed to be making a play for Adam too – I decided to admit defeat gracefully.

Tony walked in, his jacket casually slung over one shoulder.

"Where have you been, Tony?" Peter asked. "I was worried."

"No need. I just enjoyed myself at lunchtime. I watched

the lesson, though. I was hiding up in a tree in case Hewit saw me and made me join in!" Tony laughed, but Peter just looked angry.

"That's stupid behavior from someone your age. I suggest you stay in tonight." He turned his back on Tony. "Okay, the rest of you squeeze into the jeep." Peter hustled us out the door.

To my surprise, Adam seemed to go to some lengths to make sure he sat next to me on the way to bowling. He was looking great in a faded blue cotton shirt and Levi's 501s. The nearness of Adam was pleasant and somehow reassuring, and I couldn't stop myself smiling as a little shiver of happiness ran down my spine.

We ate too much pizza and at first no one felt much like bowling, but Peter had booked it and he was determined to get his money's worth. We had two of the six alleys in the large, echoing room that smelled of old bowling shoes. An electronic display board that kept score, and told you when to bowl, operated each one. At first we were all hopeless, except for Adam who seemed to be one of those infuriating people who are naturally good at any sport. After a while we got the hang of it and I even managed to win a verbal bet with Peter, who bet me I couldn't knock all the pins down with one roll.

On the way home, Adam sat next to me again, but this time he didn't talk. He just stared out of the window and I thought he must have gotten fed up with me already. After a while I felt his hand, cool and dry, find mine. He held it for a while, still staring fixedly out of the window and still saying nothing. This was probably just as well because I doubt I could have answered him sensibly. My mind was all over the place. Partly I was shy because I hadn't held hands with a boy since elementary school, and partly I was thrilled because it was Adam, handsome, much coveted Adam, who was doing the holding! I hoped that the rest of our party could see. Especially Melanie Rogers!

# chapter nine

The next day we were split into smaller groups to continue our training in different areas. Clare, Julie and I were told to go to the indoor ring to work on our dressage with Peter, while Adam, Melanie and Tony did grids out in the paddock with Captain Hewit. After a few minutes the big doors to the ring were pulled back and Adam stood there holding Custar.

"The Captain says I'm to swap with Clare this morning," he announced. Peter looked suspicious but told Clare to get a move on, and Adam mounted Custar and joined our schooling session. Peter made us work very hard. He had us trotting and cantering circles, figure eights and serpentines for about half an hour before we had a breather. He was trying to make our transitions from trot to canter *fluent and seamless* (his words, not mine) which I took to mean smooth and not jerky. While we got our breath back Peter started to explain how we could pick up better marks in a test just by being very accurate with our movements.

"If a test says trot at C, then you must trot at C, not a stride before or a stride after. Now, can you all remember the Horse Trials A test? You must have ridden it hundreds of times, but I'll call out the movements for anyone who's forgetful. I want you each to ride it in turn and the other two can make suggestions as to how to improve it." Peter went to the end of the school and pretended to be the judge.

Adam went first and Julie I stood at the edge and watched. We were supposed to be looking for faults in the test, but I soon lost concentration and began to think about Adam. He looked so good on Custar, tall and strong. He rode with a nice straight spine, his shoulders thrown back as he sat to Custar's bouncy, athletic stride. He wore leather chaps over his blue denim jeans and his black shirt had a tear in one shoulder. You could just see his tanned skin beneath. Custar turned up the centerline and halted, Adam saluted at Peter to mark the end of the test.

"Right then, Paula, stop daydreaming and tell me what was wrong with that performance." Peter fixed me with his piercing gaze.

I opened my mouth to speak but I realized I had nothing constructive to say. I couldn't remember a thing about the test, except how gorgeous Adam had looked, and I thought I'd better not say that! I dredged my brain helplessly for inspiration and came up with, "Well, his halt was a little ragged, not very square to the center line." My voice *sounded* calm enough.

"Absolutely right. A good halt at the beginning and the end of a test can make all the difference to the overall impression of the partnership. What else, Julie?"

"He let Custar fall in on some of the corners. His canter transitions were both a bit late, and he used his voice when he lengthened Custar's stride." At least one of us was paying attention!

"Yes, you'll lose marks for using your voice at any time during the test. Julie's right about the corners, Adam. He must *flow* around in a balanced rhythm, not appear to break in two at the shoulders. And remember, prepare for your transition; Custar was late only because you forgot to ask him in time. You're next Paula."

I tried as hard as I could to ride a smooth and accurate test. Jazz was listening to me, and I remembered to take my time and set him up for each transition. When we'd finished I let out a huge sigh of relief and I realized that I had been holding my breath for a long time.

"Comments, you two," Peter called to Adam and Julie.

"Her circles were a little egg shaped, but apart from that very good," said Julie.

"It was very accurate, but she looked incredibly tense," said Adam.

"I noticed that. What's the matter Paula? You usually manage to appear so relaxed." Peter seemed puzzled.

"I was probably trying too hard. I still don't completely trust Jazz not take things into his own hands. I'll have to practice looking relaxed even when I'm not!" I laughed, but I was surprised that my frame of mind had been so obvious. The *real* reason was that it suddenly seemed so important that I should make a good impression on Adam.

Julie went next and Adam and I stood together, so close that our knees were touching. Our horses sniffed at each other's noses and Jazz nibbled Custar's reins.

"I made it up about the Captain wanting Clare in his group so that I could be with you all day," Adam whispered.

"Pay attention, you two," Peter had hearing like a bat! We did as we were told, but the pressure of Adam's knee against mine was distracting. When Julie had finished we decided that she needed to practice keeping Foxy rounder during her canter to trot transitions and that she needed to keep her own head up. Apart from that she had ridden a very neat test, and she and Foxy seemed to have a sympathetic partnership, which is, after all, what it's all about.

After lunch (vegetarian pot pie followed by yummy apple pie), the Captain took us for cross-country practice again, this time to concentrate on riding combination fences. Our horses seemed to know what was coming and they jogged and bucked as we made our way down to the far end of the estate. We passed a pair of pheasants picking their way across a cornfield. I have always associated pheasants with summer rides, and I love to see their jaunty tails of rusty red feathers that shine golden in the sun.

Tony rode up beside Adam and cast a cloud over my sunny mood.

"Have you seen the size of that coffin jump, Paula?" he said, "That'll give Jazz the Wonder Horse something to think about. If he runs away with you through there you'll be in trouble."

"You don't need to sound so pleased about it," I replied, wishing that Tony would just leave me alone and not talk to me.

He was right, though, it did look scary, but I didn't need him to undermine my confidence, especially when I was starting to trust Jazz a little. The first element was a solid single rail made from an old telephone pole, followed by a huge, wood lined ditch that looked like a coffin and gave the jump its name. There was a single stride before the second rail, and that was at least a yard high.

The Captain was waiting for us in the estate's old blue jeep.

"Ride 'em in, everyone," he called, "then, when you're ready come over those logs."

He pointed to a line of four logs placed in a zigzag. I was the first to try them and I headed for the middle of each so that Jazz didn't have to keep changing his stride. He bounced cleverly through the combination like a dolphin bounces in and out of the waves. I was laughing with the sheer joy of it and I could sense that Tony was watching. Jazz seemed to catch my frivolous mood and he started bucking. I shot forward in the saddle and I almost lost my seat, managing to hang on by the skin of my teeth. The Captain called me over.

"You should have been ready for that, Paula. It's not as if he's never done it before. Now go again, and if he feels as though he's going to buck, for goodness sake sit tight and ride him through it."

I did as I was told and this time Jazz didn't buck.

When we'd all warmed up over the logs Captain Hewit (or the Walking Textbook, as Adam called him) talked us through our approach to the dreaded coffin.

"Any combination with an open ditch in it is potentially dangerous," he began, "but only if you don't set your horse up properly to jump it. Horses sometimes don't jump ditches well because they don't see them until it's too late. You must be in control as you approach, *not* galloping flat out. That's when accidents happen. Jump in on a strong but fairly short stride (allow the horse a look but don't lose any impulsion), hop over the ditch, and then send him on strongly to jump the second rail. Tony, James is the most experienced horse here. Will you go first, please."

Despite me willing him to mess it up they jumped it in textbook style and cantered back to the group. In fact, all the horses jumped it well, but it was Jazz that the Captain singled out for special praise.

"Did you see how *clever* he was through that fence?" he asked the rest of them, enthusiastically. "He made it look so easy."

My moment of glory was crushed when I saw the jealous look that Tony was giving us. Maybe for the first time he was beginning to see Jazz as serious competition.

"You may think you have a good horse," Tony whispered to me nastily, "but it doesn't mean you're a good rider." He pushed passed me and rode James aggressively away, out of the field and back in the direction of the stables.

"Where are you going?" The Captain shouted at Tony's

retreating back, but he didn't get a reply. "That boy is a good rider, but he's got a really bad attitude and the wrong temperament to be around horses," he sighed. "Let's rest the horses for twenty minutes. It's very hot."

He handed out some cookies and some bottles of water, so we jumped off and loosened our girths, giving our horses a much-needed break.


The Captain drove the long way around to the next field, but we lined our horses up waiting for our turn to jump a small, narrow stile, which was quicker than using the gate. Julie, behind me, was the last to go. As the others galloped away Foxy got excited and started rearing, disconcertingly close to the low branches.

"Stop it, Foxy!" Julie sounded nervous.

"Go in front if you want, Julie. Jazz is behaving for once!"

I held Jazz back and let Julie go first, but as Foxy charged up to the jump a large stone seemed to appear from nowhere. It skimmed the top pole and landed between Foxy's legs. He misjudged the jump completely and hit the solid rail hard, turning a somersault and catapulting Julie from the saddle. I screamed when I saw Foxy land on his side and roll toward Julie who lay horribly still beneath the fence. He struggled to his feet, and by some miracle managed to miss his rider. Left by himself in the wrong field Jazz began to panic. Desperately, I looked for a low place in the hedge and scrambled him over it. Captain Hewit and I got to Julie at the same time. Her eyes were open and she lay on her back, strangely twisted and limp looking. The Captain knelt beside her.

"Keep very still, Julie, and tell us what hurts." His tone was unrecognizably gentle and he held her hand.

"I'm not sure," Julie mumbled, "I hurt all over. I feel so stupid. It was such a silly fence to fall at. Is Foxy all right?" I looked over to Clare who was holding the bay gelding.

"Yes, Clare's got him. He looks shaken, but he seems all right."

"Does anyone have a cell phone on them?" Captain Hewit asked.

We all shook our heads.

"No? And stupidly, mine's in my car back at the yard."

The Captain was looking at the strange angle of Julie's left leg and he seemed to make a decision.

"Okay, Adam, Mel and Clare get those horses back to the stables and make them comfortable. We don't want them in the way when the ambulance comes. Paula, stay here with Julie and keep her talking. Don't let her move an inch. I'm going to phone for help." He ran to the jeep and was gone in a cloud of thick blue diesel smoke.

"Will you be all right by yourself, Paula?" Adam sounded concerned. "I'll wait with you if you like." I did like, but it seemed silly to make a fuss when Julie was lying there so badly hurt.

"No, you go with the others. Come back as soon as you can, though." He smiled his agreement and was gone, riding Custar and leading Jazz. I turned back to Julie.

"I'm sorry to be such a nuisance," she said, trying to sound brave.

"Don't worry, you're not being. It could've happened to any of us. Are you warm enough?"

"Yes thank you. I can't remember what happened though. Did I fall off?"

"Yes, Foxy turned over. You were lucky he didn't land on you."

I took her hand like the Captain had and was reassured to find it was warm and dry, not cold and clammy as I'd expected. Julie spoke again.

"Did I fall off? I can't remember a thing."

I thought she hadn't heard me the first time, so I repeated what I'd seen of the accident.

Julie looked up at me thoughtfully, "Oh, I see," she said, "I can't remember a thing... did I fall off?"

A horrible chill went through my whole body as I realized that Julie was losing her memory. Again I told her what had happened, she listened intently, and then asked again if she'd fallen off. This time she asked where she was, too.

I talked to her endlessly, repeating myself over and over again in as normal a way as I could. I felt very much alone and horribly stiff, crouched as I was, still holding Julie's hand. I glanced at my watch. The hands had hardly moved since the last time I'd looked. I prayed the ambulance would come soon.

"Did I fall off? I can't remember a thing." Julie asked for the hundredth time. I felt like changing my story, telling her she'd been run down by a herd of elephants, anything to break the eerie monotony of this strange and frightening situation.

I heard an unusual noise overhead. It got louder and louder, a frantic chugging, flapping sort of noise.

"It's the Air Ambulance, Julie!" I shouted above the din.

It hovered into sight like a big, red insect, circling around us to find a place to land. An unexplained rush of adrenalin swept through me as I watched the helicopter land with the precision of a butler laying cups for a tea party. Grinning stupidly, I protected Julie's body from the man-made gale until the rotors slowed, the paramedics decanted from their craft and a kind of peace settled on the scene once again.

"Right then, honey, what have you been up to?" The ambulance man was a large, unfit looking individual with a boisterous cheerfulness that must have been particularly useful in his line of work. His partner came over carrying a folded metal stretcher. He was a gloomy looking character with a long, pessimistic face. Ever so slowly and ever so gently they began their examination, questioning Julie and questioning me.

Captain Hewit's sports car came into sight, bouncing alarmingly as it went through the dusty gateway. I was especially glad to see Adam in the passenger seat.

"We'd have been here sooner," Adam explained, "but the jeep wouldn't start!"

When it came to getting her onto the stretcher we all had to help. Adam had the job of holding her head and neck still while the rest of us maneuvered the two halves of the stretcher beneath her. She needed gas and air, administered by the gloomy one, to help her with the pain of being moved. Her agonizing cries became uneasy giggles as the gas did its work. I found the whole experience completely unnerving. The Captain went with Julie in the helicopter and told Adam to take care of me.

"A ride in a helicopter is almost worth getting smashed up for," said Adam as we stood watching the decreasing red dot in the sky.

Captain Hewit seemed to have forgotten about his car. Gesturing toward it, Adam put his arm around my shoulders and asked me,

"Do you want to walk back, or ride in style?"

"Captain Hewit would be furious!"

"We can't just leave it here in the middle of the field," Adam said reasonably.

"Well, how do I know you can drive?"

"Of course I can drive. All farmers' sons can. It's a natural instinct that's in our genes. Come on, I'll show you."

He took my hand and led me toward the car. I sat in the deep leather seat, feeling warm and very comfortable in Adam's company, though still a little shy.

To my relief he handled the little car confidently and I began to relax and enjoy myself. Then my mind went back to the accident. I couldn't work out where the stone had come from.

"Did *you* see what happened?" I asked Adam.

"No. Clare, Melanie and I had a race across the field. Clare thinks that's what made Foxy get in such a tizzy.

She's crying a river about it now, saying it's all our fault."

"That didn't make him fall," I said, "it was a stone that practically tripped him up. It just appeared over the jump. I saw it with my own eyes, but it still doesn't make any sense to me."

"Maybe Tony can shed some light on it," said Adam thoughtfully as he negotiated a narrow gateway, "For some reason he was hanging around by the jump when I went over it. He disappeared pretty quickly... I thought it was because he saw Hewit coming."

"I didn't see him. I wonder what he came back for. And why didn't he stay to help when he saw that Julie was hurt? I bet he had his phone on him."

"Maybe he's squeamish," said Adam.

*And maybe I'm going to be the next Queen of England*, I said, but not out loud.

None of us felt much like going out that night. We all helped Peter cook dinner and then sat quietly around the big pine table, eating but probably not tasting our chicken and fries. We had had no news from the hospital, except that Julie was undergoing examinations and tests, but for what we didn't dare even think about. The phone rang and made us all jump.

"I'll get it," said Peter.

When he came back he was looking more relaxed.

"Well, she's not in any danger, but she is a bit banged up. She has a broken pelvis and a cracked bone in her neck. Both are pretty bad, but she'll recover in time." He looked grave, "I still don't understand how it happened. Are you *sure* none of you were fooling around?"

We had been through it over and over again. Tony insisted he hadn't seen anything, so I was no nearer discovering the origin of the stone.

"If there *was* a stone," Tony looked at me meaningfully, "Maybe one of the other horses kicked it out of the wall."

The others thought this the most likely explanation, but I wasn't convinced. The direction was wrong, to begin with, and anyway the stone had been too large and too heavy. I was fairly sure that Tony had thrown it himself, but why? What had he to gain from injuring Julie? There was something not right about the whole affair, but I couldn't quite put my finger on it.

We were all exhausted and went to bed early. Adam said goodnight to me at the foot of the stairs, with such a slow and lingering hug that I was sorry when it came to an end and we went our separate ways. My head was spinning with thoughts of Julie and thoughts of Adam. Sleep, when it came, was fitful, and I tossed and turned between the starched, white sheets.

# chapter ten

I woke up in the middle of the night and sat bolt upright. Everything suddenly made sense; Tony must have thought that I was behind Clare, not Julie. He seemed to think he had plenty of reasons to get at me. We'd never liked each other even before I'd insulted his mother and gotten him expelled from school, and now he seemed to be jealous of Jazz. I sank back down again. It was all very well suspecting it, but proving it would be a different matter. I wasn't sure that I wanted to prove it either. The less I had to do with Tony the better I liked it, and it wouldn't turn the clock back and help Julie.

I lay awake for hours going over things in my head. When I managed to stop thinking about Tony for a few seconds I found myself thinking about Bella and the horrific attack on her. Could he have been involved in that, too? Eventually I saw the sky turn from inky black to gray and heard the first tentative bird song, the overture to the dawn chorus.

*It's no good*, I told myself, *I might as well get up*. I dressed and went out to the stables. Jazz was surprised to see me and delighted when I gave him the remains of an old candy bar that I found in my pocket. Some people are easily pleased! I left him licking his teeth and making faces.

It was a wonderful morning. The gray dawn light had gone and now the sky was a watery blue. My feet left a trail in the dew as I ran across the fields, heading for the spot where Julie had fallen. I suddenly noticed that mine weren't the only tracks; someone else had been that way before me, and as far as I could tell, they hadn't returned. I froze in my stride, unreasonably scared. Ahead was a twisted, old oak tree that I guessed I could easily climb. Its branches would hide and protect me; I shinnied up it quickly and sat very still, waiting to see who would return. Minutes passed but no one came. I climbed higher, trying to see beyond the first field and out toward the jump. I was right up in the canopy of the tree, much higher than my tree house at home.

It was then that I made the mistake of looking down.

"Ooh," I felt decidedly sick. Both the ground and the tree seemed to be moving. I looked again but the earth just swam before my eyes. I fixed my gaze rigidly in front of me and tried to find a lower branch with my foot. It slipped.

"Oh, no!" Now I was feeling dizzy as well as sick.

Below me I could hear footsteps but I dared not look down. The footsteps stopped, then started anew, as if someone was walking around the bottom of my tree. I knew I was well hidden by the thick foliage, but I hugged the branch tightly for comfort. Then, to my horror I heard and felt the unmistakable noises and vibrations of someone climbing the tree beneath me. Louder and louder, breathing and grunting, twigs cracking.

*This is it*, I said to myself, *I'm a sitting duck. Tony just has to tip me out of the tree and it will look like an accident.*

I shut my eyes against the tears and waited for the shove.

"Paula, it that you? What on earth are you doing up there?" It was Adam's voice. I thought I was going crazy.

I allowed myself a peep and to my enormous relief saw the dark, curly top of Adam's head. The world spun so I shut my eyes tightly again.

It took Adam an hour to talk me down from that tree. I was pathetic. Not one measure of my body or brain worked properly, so he gave me instructions, inch by inch, in a calm, matter of fact voice that I intuitively knew I could trust. Toward the bottom I was all right again but I was enjoying his firm grip on my legs so I pretended I wasn't. We walked slowly back. Adam put his arm around me and I felt extremely grateful to be safely out of that horrible tree.

"Now," he said, turning toward me, "are you going to tell me *why* you were up there?"

I told him everything, right from the beginning, except for what had happened to Bella. The Police had been very insistent that no one else should know. I started with Tony setting me up to look like a thief in front of his mother and finished with my suspicions about him throwing the rock. He listened without interruption, and then started to chuckle.

101

"Tony told me that you were not to be trusted, said something about stuff going missing when you'd ridden for his mom."

"What?" I was furious, "The lying toad. He more or less admitted he'd set me up. He said that I couldn't prove anything," I stormed.

"It's all right, calm down, I didn't believe him for a second. There was a guy like him who used to work for my dad. He was always taking off early and blaming other people when his work wasn't done properly. I had my suspicions about Tony myself after yesterday. I came out early this morning to see if I could shed any light on it," he paused for breath, "and do you know what?"

"What?" I asked.

"There was a big stone lying on the ground just before the take off, *and*, on further investigation..."

"Get on with it, Sherlock," I prompted.

"On further investigation of the hedge, next to where Tony was standing, I found a stone-shaped hole..." he was being infuriatingly slow for maximum dramatic effect.

"And the stone that you found fits the hole," I concluded for him.

"Exactly, my dear Watson, moss and all. Trouble is, it still doesn't prove anything, but I'm fairly sure that is what happened, and you may be right in thinking that the accident should have been yours."

I shuddered; it was horrible to think it could so easily have been me lying in a hospital bed.

When we reached the yard there was a lot of activity; Peter came out from Jazz's stall with an empty bucket.

"I've fed your nags, and I *won't* ask what you've been getting up to because I don't want to have to tell your father about it, Paula!" He was smiling – luckily.

"I'd like to know *what* you can get *up* to, thirty feet up an oak tree," Adam said, with some feeling.

"Just hurry up, now that you're here. Breakfast will be ready in ten minutes and then your parents will be arriving to take you home, thank goodness! The responsibility is getting to me!"

"Adam," I called him into Jazz's stall, "don't say anything to Tony. We don't *know* that he did it and it won't help Julie now."

More to the point, I was scared of the repercussions.

"OK," he said simply, "we'll let sleeping dogs lie... I'll be watching him, though!"

# chapter eleven

After the excitement of the course, home seemed very dull, though Bella seemed pleased to see us, well, Jazz anyway. She called to him when she heard hooves in the yard and came to look over her half door. It was the most interest I'd seen her take in anything since her attack. Outwardly her wounds were healing, though she'd be left with scars, but inwardly she'd changed. She was no longer affectionate; it was if she couldn't trust anyone not to hurt her.

"Poor Bella, you've had a horrible time. Things *will* get better, though," I told her, smoothing her neck and feeding her crumbs from my pocket. Sadly, I thought of her foal that wouldn't be born and wondered what color it might have been. The foal would have cheered her up and given her something to live for.

Ellan chose that moment to bike into the yard.

"Hello!" I was especially glad to see her – I wanted to tell *someone* about Adam.

We made sandwiches and filled a thermos with ice-cold lemonade that we took to my tree house for an impromptu picnic. Ellan listened patiently.

"He's got dark, wavy hair, brown eyes, really broad shoulders..." I droned on and on, forgetting that Ellan had seen him at Charmley.

I gave her a sidelong glance to see if this information surprised her at all. She wasn't surprised, but there was *something* different about her. She smoothed a stray lock of hair behind one ear. It was a darker, richer color than usual and cut in a modern, spiky style.

"Ellan! Your hair, it's gorgeous... and you've had your ears pierced! You lucky thing. Dad won't even talk about letting me have mine done since Freya did hers with a sewing needle. She was thirteen at the time, but he still hasn't forgiven her. There are kids in nursery school that have their ears pierced nowadays, but Dad still says I'm too young."

I felt a stab of jealousy. Ellan's parents let her do tons of things I wasn't allowed to do, but like my parents, they'd always said *no* to ear piercing.

"Mom was fed up with me going on about how young I look compared to you and everyone else at school. It's rotten being so small. *Everyone* is more developed than I am! Having my hair done was the only thing we could think of that might make me look more sophisticated. Then when the hairdresser had finished she suggested earrings, and mom just agreed, no fuss!" She shook her head merrily and the tiny gold studs twinkled.

"They're gorgeous! Maybe Dad will let *me* now – and maybe Bella will sprout wings!"

"But that's not all," said Ellan, hardly able to stop herself grinning, "When I was waiting in the jewelers to have them done, there was this really cute boy waiting for his mother, and he asked me out to the movies this Friday." She glowed at the thought. "And, do you know what else? He thought I was at *least* fifteen!"

I was sitting by the phone, two days later, with a crumpled up piece of paper clutched in my hand. On it was written Adam's phone number. It wasn't the first time I'd sat there, trying to pluck up the courage to call him. I'd spent a miserable couple of days willing him to call me and I was feeling kind of lonely. Jazz was having a rest, Ellan was wrapped up with her new boyfriend, Jason, and even Luke was busy. He'd discovered the television and had been glued to it ever since, much to Freya's consternation.

Freya came and joined me by the phone.

"What's up? Hasn't he phoned?" she asked.

I shook my head sadly and stuck my bottom lip out. I was doing an impression of Luke when scolded. Freya laughed.

"Men! Why ever do we bother with them? Peter hasn't phoned me either, not for a whole week. I know he's been busy competing, but all the same. Why don't we go and have some lemonade, with chocolate chip cookies... and a good cry?"

As we got up to go the phone rang. I grabbed it.

"Hello... Adam!"

"Oh well," said Freya, stoically, "tears and cookies for one!"

I was on the bus to Redchester within the hour. Adam met me outside the Town Hall and swept me off my feet like they do in the films.

"I've got the afternoon off from hay-making," he announced, "The baler's broken and it'll take the rest of the day to fix it."

"Do you *have* to work on the farm?" I asked him.

"If I want to keep Custar and go to events and training sessions, I do. Dad pays me and it's fun, actually. Trouble is, it doesn't leave me much time to take beautiful girls out to lunch."

"It's a good thing you don't know any, then, isn't it?" I answered, blushing at the compliment.

We had a late lunch at Jane's. It was full of middle-aged couples having the Early-Bird special. I wondered if, in years to come, Adam and I would end up like them. We ordered the Dish of the Day, which was macaroni cheese and salad. We talked so easily. There weren't any awkward silences, just a few comfortable ones when we had our mouths too full of macaroni to converse politely.

"We'll go and visit Julie in the hospital first, and then we can go to the park," Adam said, when at last we felt we'd overstayed our welcome at the restaurant.

He paid the bill and we walked, his arm across my shoulders, down the main street.

The hospital overlooked the town. It was a stone building without decoration or character, and we found Julie's room at the end of an echoing, pale green corridor. She was lying flat on her back, small and clean in a starched bed. Her neck was braced and we had to stand up and look down in order to speak to her. Despite all this she seemed remarkably cheerful.

"Hello, it's great to see you both," she beamed at us.

Adam placed the chocolates we'd brought next to her bed.

"Silly question, but how are you feeling?" I asked her.

"Not *too* bad. At least I'm not in pain. It's boring more than anything."

I looked around, not knowing what to say. I noticed a huge bunch of expensive looking flowers on her table.

"What beautiful flowers. Are they from your Mom and Dad?"

"No," she blushed, "they're from Tony. There's a card too, and he's phoned me every day."

*So, he does have a conscience!* I thought to myself.

"Can you remember how the accident happened?" Adam asked.

"Not really, I just remember Foxy stumbling before the jump. He didn't stand a chance after that. It wasn't his fault."

"It was the stone that tripped him," I told her, "Did *you* see where it came from?"

"There wasn't a stone, he just tripped," she said firmly.

"But I *saw* it," I was confused now, though still sure of what I'd seen.

"Paula," she said crossly, "there *wasn't* a stone." Her voice had an unfamiliar edge to it. We held each other's gaze for a few seconds before I turned away. I looked across at Adam. He knew there had been a stone. Almost imperceptibly Adam shook his head at me.

"OK," I said, to Julie, "no stone."

If she didn't want there to be a stone, then that was fine by me, but I was grateful when the visit was cut short by a bustling nurse, "I'm taking Julie for physical therapy now," she said.

It was good to be out of the dry, stifling heat and artificial light of the hospital. We headed toward the park and took a shortcut down a narrow alleyway. We stopped to look in a shop window that was full of bric-a-brac, piled high on every available space and covered with a thin layer of dust. *Gibson's Antiques, Collectibles and Objets D'Art* was written in gold leaf across the glass. The window display was fascinating. It contained items that neither Adam nor I had ever seen before and we giggled about their possible uses. Then my eye was caught by something I did recognize. Right at the back, half hidden under a forty-eight star flag, was a little metal horse. It stood around four inches tall, its haunches were low as if it was about to spring forward and its head was turned to look at us. Adam saw it too.

"Isn't he *beautiful*. He looks like your Jazz. I think it's the way his mouth is open and he looks as though he's about to do something awful."

I hit him for this slur on my nice horse's character. He was right, though. There was something about the little figure that reminded me of Jazz. Maybe it was something to do with the well-muscled body or the arrogant turn of his head.

"Let's go inside and see how much he is," I said, opening the door that rang a bell in the back of the shop. The inside was just like the window, except there was even more dust. An elderly man in a clean white apron came to greet us; it had to be Mr. Gibson himself.

"Good afternoon, Madam, Sir, how may I assist you?" His voice was slow and deliberate.

I began to giggle, but Adam nudged me and said, "The model horse in your window. We'd like a closer look at it, please."

"Ah, the Brazen Horse, an excellent choice."

Trader Gibson took a huge bunch of keys from his belt and unlocked the door to his shop window. I wondered how he knew which was the right key from amongst so many. He moved nimbly through his display and found the horse beneath the faded flag. He was a small, thin, gray sort of man, but he had the innocent smile of a child and he handed the horse to me with a look of real tenderness for the little figurine.

"Do you know the story behind it?" he asked and we shook our heads. "The original Brazen Horse was a gift to the King of Sarra from the King of Arabia. He was not only beautiful but magic too. All the King had to do was touch a golden pin in the horse's ear and the beast would carry him anywhere. Look, there's the pin," he pointed a long, bony finger to a tiny knot of metal in the horse's ear that looked to me like a mistake in the casting.

"Of course, the gold leaf has worn off it now, but what do you expect from such a venerable piece?"

I held the exquisite little horse and ran my hands over its smooth, dark surface. He was very heavy and the worn metal gleamed in the low light.

"How much is he?" I asked.

"Twenty dollars, but I could let you have him for fifteen."

My brain began to work overtime. I had twenty dollars in my pocket, given to me by Dad for emergencies, but he would expect most of that back when I got home. I didn't think he'd see this as an emergency somehow.

"How would it be if we went halves on it?" said Adam. "Ten bucks each. You could keep it at your house, then I'd have to keep coming over to visit you to keep an eye on my investment."

I agreed; owning half of the Brazen Horse with Adam was even better than owning all of him by myself. It seemed to lend a pleasing, long-term aspect to our relationship. Mr. Gibson wrapped the horse lovingly in soft tissue paper and then placed him in a sturdy cardboard box. He handed him to me and said, "He really is a magic horse, you know. I didn't make the story up."

"I wish my horse had a golden pin in his ear that would make him do what I want," I said, with feeling. "Nothing else seems to!"

We went to the park and played on the swings like a couple of ten year olds. Then we sat on a bench and made plans.

"There's Tidmount in two weekends and Berncarrow two weekends after that," said Adam.

"We'll be back at school by then. What an awful thought."

"At least neither of us has SATs this year," said Adam cheerily.

He was going to be a junior this year. I didn't have major exams for another two years.

"I wish we went to the same school," I lamented, "then we could see each other every day. You could protect me from Tony Frost. That's if he's allowed *back* in school this year."

"I've got to go soon," Adam whispered, "let's not waste time talking about school."

It was warm in the park, but not too warm to enjoy the closeness of Adam as he put his arms around my waist.

# chapter twelve

Freya crunched the gears and braked jerkily as we drove through the wide gates of Tidmount House and followed the signs to the horse trailer park. After a lot of soul searching Dad had entrusted her with his car. There was one major advantage in it for him; a Saturday that he didn't have to spend at a horse event with me. It was just getting light and we had been on the road for nearly two hours.

"Wake up, Paula, we're here." She nudged me with her elbow and I forced my eyes to open wide and wondered what it was that made me trek all over the county at unreasonable hours of the day and night, chasing rosettes.

The fresh air revived me. It was cold and very autumnal. Somewhere deep inside I had a feeling of rising excitement that I kept pushing down and squashing. At first I thought it was competition nerves, but as I woke up I realized that it was because Adam was also riding at Tidmount and I would see him for the first time since the day we'd bought the Brazen Horse. I'd brought the little model with me to bring us luck. After all, Mr. Gibson had said it was magic.

Freya walked the cross-country course with me and I ran and skipped all the way until she got annoyed and told me to concentrate and that I'd wear myself out before the riding began. The course looked huge. Most of the jumps seemed way over the maximum height allowed for the class, although Freya assured me that they weren't. There was a water jump, two banks and a wide ditch with a rail over the top. Suddenly I decided that I didn't care. The sun was shining, Jazz was a star and very soon I'd be seeing Adam! Life seemed pretty good. I turned to my sister, gave her my best smile and listened intently to her advice on how to ride the course.

I met Adam outside the refreshment tent, (a pre-arranged rendezvous), at eight thirty. We had exactly ten minutes together before we both had to rush back to ride our horses before the dressage. I felt shy at first and I think he did too. For a few minutes neither of us could think what to say and then we both began talking at once.

"Sorry," said Adam, ever the gentleman, "what were you going to say?"

"I was only going to ask where your Dad parked the truck. We could ask Freya to move our trailer nearby."

"That's a good idea. We can have lunch and everything together. Why don't I come back with you now and we'll persuade her to move."

Adam took my hand and led me across the park. I felt self-conscious when we met up with Freya, but she didn't look particularly surprised and she agreed to move as long as I got up on Jazz that very minute and warmed him up.

"Your dressage is in less than an hour, and then you're show jumping thirty minutes after that. Now get a *move* on. You can see Adam later."

Jazz's mane looked unusually elegant with ten neat little braids down his neck. He was very excited and spun around in circles when I tried to mount, which made me feel giddy. I worked for about thirty minutes, trying to remember all the things I'd learned on the course. When I was satisfied I patted his neck and took him back to Freya.

"Here, put your jacket on, and your gloves." Freya bossed me around for a while, and then legged me up on Jazz and told me to take him around the horse lines so that he got used to his surroundings. He felt very excited, and he jogged and snatched at the reins, threatening to buck. I tried to relax and reassure him, but I was tense, and as my tension relayed itself to Jazz he fussed all the more. I took him back to Freya.

"He feels terrifying. I'm expecting him to do something awful with every stride," I whined.

My nerves had begun to jangle and Freya looked concerned.

"Don't let him get to you, Paula. Just go and enjoy yourself."

"Good luck, Paula," Adam called to me from somewhere underneath Custar. He was putting studs into the dun's back shoes, but he raised his arm in a friendly wave as I passed and I began to relax a little.

I kept Jazz around the dressage arenas so that I would know when it was my turn. His long stride felt impressively elevated and I was vaguely aware of several admiring spectators watching him. When the judge gave me the signal to start, Jazz puffed himself up even more and the space inside the arena seemed to shrink. We started off well, trotting a perfectly shaped circle and lengthening our stride powerfully across the diagonal. I was beginning to enjoy myself as he steadied for the corner and I half halted before asking him to canter left. However, instead of striking off into canter, in one movement Jazz left the arena and reared, towering above the judge's stand. We seemed to stay up in the air for hours and my feet swung precariously free of the long, dressage length stirrups. When we came back down to earth I kicked Jazz hard to show him my displeasure. I took him back into the arena and continued the test, trying desperately to put the incident behind me. The next three minutes felt like thirty, but somehow we finished without further incident. Instead of smiling at the judge during my final salute I found it impossible to stop the tears that were running down my cheeks. I trotted past Freya and Adam, pretending not to see them, and took Jazz the long way back to the horse trailer. On the way we had a lengthy, rather one-sided conversation and I told him, in stern language, exactly what I thought of him. It got it off my chest and I was beginning to see the funny side of the incident when I noticed a familiar green horse trailer and Tony Frost standing on the ramp.

"Do you know," he called to me as I passed, "that horse could be great, if only you could ride him properly. I'll buy him from you, Paula. I've got five bucks on me!" He laughed as he saw my tears start again.

I hurried past, not trusting myself to speak, and headed toward the show jumping ring. The jumps seemed impossibly huge until I realized that I was allowing things to get to me.

"We can jump those stupid fences," I told Jazz as we whisked effortlessly over the practice fence. Adam trotted past me.

"Wish me luck. It's my turn next," he said.

I did, and I watched Custar try his best, giving Adam a wonderfully fluent round that made the small crowd of spectators clap in appreciation. Adam grinned and patted Custar's shiny yellow neck. As if to make up for the dressage, Jazz also produced a clear round, leaping far higher over each fence than he needed to, as though he was jumping for the sheer joy of it. I hugged his neck and patted him for a long time. He was forgiven, just!

I didn't eat much lunch. Freya had moved the trailer and we shared our food with Adam and Mr. Bray. I liked the look of Mr. Bray. He was about fifty and he had gray hair and a very tanned, craggy face with brown eyes that twinkled like Adam's did. Between mouthfuls of food, the conversation was lively and centered around politics, farming and the stock market.

"The trouble with China is..." Mr. Bray was in the

middle of enlightening us, when we all noticed that Freya had stopped mid-bite and gone a deep crimson color. We followed her gaze and saw Peter Edmund coming toward us. He covered the ground as effortlessly as one of his leggy Thoroughbreds.

"Hi!" he greeted us, "How've you two been doing?"

"Pretty good! We were both clear show jumping," I said, and then I remembered Jazz's dressage performance and my heart flopped down into my socks. "But after this morning, when Jazz reared in the dressage test, I'll have to do something pretty spectacular to get placed," I moaned.

"You might be surprised," said Peter. "The nice thing about dressage is that each movement is marked separately. You could get no marks at all for one part, but score nine for another. If the rest of the test was convincing you may get more marks than someone who did a less accurate, less inspiring test."

"Hmmm," I wasn't convinced.

"Well, if you don't believe me wait and see when the marks go up."

Peter turned his attention to Freya who, with tremendous efforts to look nonchalant, offered him a sandwich and a glass of soda.

Adam and I left them and wandered over to the secretary's van to see if the scores had been published. There was a knot of competitors around the board and I pushed my way to the front. To my surprise and delight Jazz had gotten away with an unbelievable forty eight penalties, far less than I'd expected, so Peter must have been right about the rest of his test being good. It put him into fifth place, which was very respectable. Adam was in second place behind Tony Frost. He hugged me in delight.

"We've got everything to ride for, no penalties to add after show jumping, and two fabulous, fit, eager, clever horses to ride. Jazz and Custar are both faster than Tony's James, you know," he told me.

Adam's enthusiasm was infectious. I began to forget my nerves, and the butterflies that had been doing aerobics in my stomach disappeared. We raced each other back to change into cross-country gear, shrieking with laughter as we went.

*What am I doing here?* I asked myself, as I waited at the start. The memory of the Charmley event came back to me. At least this time I felt we had much more experience and practice under our belts, as well as a stronger bit. Jazz was sweating already; he jogged on the spot, anxious to be off.

The starter turned to me and said, "I'll count you down from five, number 89... five, four, three, two, one, go. Good luck."

We were off. From the beginning I urged Jazz on. The stakes were high; a fast, clear round could easily pull us up a few places. I felt totally exhilarated as we galloped on, taking the jumps out of our stride: the rails, the barrels, sharp right turn then onto the bank. Down hill now and into the woods, over a huge fence with its wide, yawning ditch that held no fears for my brave, clever little Polish horse. I steadied him as we jumped into the quarry and then used my legs hard to send him into the coffin, one, two, three and out again. The woods were empty of spectators, so I let out a shout of pure joy to the trees as we left them once more for the open fields. After each jump I told Jazz that I loved him and he galloped for the next fence, actively seeking more fun. He touched the big stone wall with his front feet, but it didn't deter him and he gave the corner an extra foot in height to make sure. The last stretch was uphill, but as we thundered through the finish he felt as though he could have gone around again.

For the second time that day I burst into tears, this time with a mixture of relief and excitement and exhaustion and love for Jazz. We walked slowly back to the trailer and I patted him all the way and fed him mints which he gobbled greedily, almost taking my fingers with them. He was very sweaty. His thick winter coat had already started to ghost through his summer one. Gratefully, I let Freya take Jazz from me and I collapsed onto the ramp of the trailer and drank from a bottle of lukewarm orange juice.

A few seconds later Adam joined me, "Did you go clear, Paula?"

I nodded and he smiled, "Me too. We must have a chance, then. Lots of people were stopping at the coffin."

He sighed with deep satisfaction, took the orange juice from me and drank it all.

It took forever for the officials to announce the final results. A big crowd of anxious competitors had gathered around the van waiting for the sheets to be posted. A flustered woman pushed through the throng, using the scoreboard as a shield until she had room to put it up. A hush came over the gathering as everyone looked for his or her own name on the list. My knees went weak when I saw mine.

"Second!" I gasped, "and Adam, you're first. The Brazen Horse *has* brought us luck!"

I looked for Tony's name. He was third. There was just one penalty between us.

"I want to make a complaint," said a voice from behind me.

I didn't have to turn around to know it was Tony's.

"Number 89 should have been eliminated in the dressage. Her horse left the arena," he said, with great satisfaction in his voice.

"Is that right?" said a harassed course official. "Hold on a minute, everyone." He removed the board and took it back inside the caravan, "I'll have go and see about this."

"Peter," I ran to him, "is that right? Are you eliminated if you leave the arena?"

I could feel tears of utter disappointment pricking my eyes. To lose my place at this stage was bitterly cruel.

Peter put his arm around my shoulder and gently led me away, saying, "Yes, Paula hon, I'm afraid you are."

# chapter thirteen

I love Sunday mornings. There's always a gentle peacefulness about them that rarely enters into the other days of the week. Lying in bed I started to come to terms with the bitter disappointment of the day before. Bella would never have reared like Jazz had, nor would she have galloped so fast across country. Rules were rules, I kept telling myself, but it was a hard lesson to learn. It was after ten o'clock when Mom brought me a glass of juice. She went to the window and opened the curtains to let the bright, crisp morning in.

"We thought you might appreciate a lie-in," said Mom, "so Freya fed Bella and Jazz for you."

"That was nice," I stretched and yawned loudly. "It's so *great* lying in bed! Mom, do you think Freya will help me clip Jazz this morning? He got really sweaty yesterday and it's not good for him."

"I doubt it. She's going out to lunch with Peter. He's taking her and Luke to a restaurant with a children's room. She's booked the bathroom for the whole morning to get ready!" Mom laughed.

"I'll have to manage by myself then. We had a lecture on it once at the Pony Club, and it *looked* easy enough."

"I'd help, but I'm at a pretty difficult point in my painting. I want to get on with that today," Mom said, with the familiar dreamy look in her eyes that was always there when she talked about her work. "Ask Dad if you get stuck."

Freya looked gorgeous when she eventually emerged from the bathroom. Luke looked deceivingly sweet and clean too, having been scrubbed from head to foot and squeezed into his only decent pair of slacks. Freya looked doubtful when I told her I was going to clip Jazz.

"It's not as easy as it looks," she told me, "You must be very careful to keep the lead away from Jazz's feet and remember to lubricate the clippers every few minutes to cool them down."

She was in the middle of writing a list of things I should and shouldn't do when Peter's car pulled up outside. She gathered Luke up in her arms and rushed him to the door.

"Bye, have fun," I said, noticing with interest the flush that had come over Freya's face, "and Luke, behave yourself... for your Mom's sake!"

I found the clippers in a box in a corner of the garage; they hadn't been used in quite a while. I consulted Freya's list. *Use fresh blades*, it said, and *Wear overalls*. – Jazz or me?

I put on a voluminous jumpsuit, which made walking

difficult, and shuffled across to where I'd fastened Jazz. I let the clippers run for a while to see if he minded the noise, but he just turned nonchalantly away and stared wistfully in the direction of the paddock. With some trepidation I made the first cut into Jazz's thickening bay coat. The hair fell silently away, leaving his mouse-gray, healthy looking skin gleaming and exposed. He flicked an ear back but seemed quite unperturbed so I cut another line, warming to my task. I decided to give Jazz a blanket clip that would take all the hair off his neck and belly but leave his back and legs protected. I stopped clipping for a while and marked out the lines with a piece of chalk. Then, just for fun I clipped a large *J*, for Jazz, on one side of his neck and a rather crooked *P*, for Paula on the other. He sighed deeply, obviously not appreciating the joke.

I was getting on well and had taken all the hair off his belly when I tried to get a line to run straight down his side. I sneezed unexpectedly and the line jumped a couple of inches. I started again a little higher up but by this time I suppose my wrist must have been getting tired because, try as I might, I just couldn't get the line to run even.

I stood back to oil the clippers and get a proper look – I was horrified! The line ran steeply upwards toward his tail, far too high for a blanket clip, and the graffiti on his neck made him look like a Hip Hop fan.

I began to panic. In my haste to remove the *J* I clipped too near to his mane and a great line of it fell noiselessly to the floor.

It was with a mixture of horror and relief that I noticed

Peter's car pull into the driveway. Freya, Peter and Luke got out – they could hardly keep their eyes off Jazz.

"Well," said Peter, "you *are* going to create an impression at your next event!"

"Is this some kind of fashion statement?" asked Freya, who was finding it very hard to keep a straight face.

I felt like crying. I had wanted to make Jazz look good, but he just looked ridiculous. Tears pricked hotly at the back of my eyes and I turned away from them.

"Paula, don't get upset," Freya came toward me, "I can fix this. We'll just give him a full clip – he's got a good quality waterproof rug so he'll be fine."

"You *must* let me take a picture of him first," said Peter, taking his camera phone out of his pocket.

Freya put the jumpsuit on and finished Jazz off in no time, making it look easy, which I knew by then it wasn't. He looked magnificent and I made Peter take another photo. Then I took one of him with Freya and Luke sitting on the trunk of his car. I thought they looked like a very happy little family.

"Can Jason and I come and watch your next escapade? It's next Saturday, isn't it?" Ellan asked, referring to the event at Berncarrow. We were on the school bus. It was the first day of school and I was still half asleep from having to get up early to feed Jazz and Bella.

"If you *must*! It'll give Jason a laugh anyway," I said despondently.

It seemed as though I'd invested such a lot of time, energy and emotion into Jazz with nothing to show for it. We had been eliminated from our first two competitions and all I'd achieved so far were bruises, humiliation and the occasional feeling of blind terror. I didn't really relish the idea of having further humiliations witnessed by a stranger.

"I'm warning you, though, if you laugh when I fall off I'll..." I racked my brain for a threat dire enough to work, "I'll... I know, I'll tell Jason about the teddy bear you still sleep with!"

Ellan and I met that evening, this time on our ponies, at our usual place, half way between her house and mine. Rikki and Jazz knew each other well and trotted along happily together while we chatted.

"I'm in cute Mr. Atkins' class for English," said Ellan dreamily.

"You don't like *him,* do you?" I was aghast.

"Well, I used to, but not so much now that I have Jason. Want to go up the hill for a canter?" Ellan suggested.

"Yes, OK. How's Rikki's jumping coming?" I asked her.

"Pretty well. I use your method with the lunge rope and make him jump anything new by himself. After I've seen him go over, it gives me the confidence to make him do it with me on top."

"So you'll be entering all the Pony Club competitions next year, then?"

"Oh yeah! I can just see Mrs. Harvey's face when I tell her that I'm going to lunge Rikki around the jumps before I get on him! 'Oh, no Ellan, dear, that's *not* in the Pony

Club rules!'" Ellan gasped in a mock stage whisper, which was just like Mrs. Harvey's.

"Do you think your mom would lend us her digital camera to film a schooling session?" I asked, "I've read that it's really good for improving your riding; seeing all your horrible faults on screen."

"I don't dare talk to mom about borrowing the camera, not after our *documentary* effort!" Ellan started to giggle at the memory.

"Do you remember Licorice's face?" I chuckled, "and your mom's, for that matter. I don't know who looked more surprised!"

We giggled uncontrollably and our ponies caught our mood. Almost as one they kicked up their heels and galloped us up to the top of the hill.


"Hello, Ellan, yes Paula's here, I'll just get her," Mom passed the phone across the kitchen table to me. It was Friday night and I was feeling very cheerful, with the whole weekend stretched luxuriously out in front of me. Mom continued making pastry.

"Hi, what's up?" I guessed that something must be because we'd been gabbing on the school bus an hour before.

"It's Rikki, he's messing me up again. I built this weird looking brush jump in the paddock and he's refusing to even consider jumping it. Can you come over? I need an extra pair of hands." Her voice sounded wavery, as if she wasn't far away from crying.

"I'll be over in ten minutes," I assured her.

Mom put the pie she'd been making in the oven and dusted her floury hands on her apron.

"Is Ellan having trouble with Rikki again? Poor thing, I do feel sorry for her. She's such a little person and he bullies her!" Mom said sympathetically.

"Don't let Ellan hear you calling her little. Anyway, Jazz bullies me too. It's part of the fun of having horses. Can I take a sandwich and go over? I'll be back before dark."

"I'll make it, you go and change," said my wonderful mother, "Is ham and cheese all right?"

I biked to Ellan's house, one hand on the handlebars, the other clutching my sandwich. She was waiting for me outside the paddock gate.

"Thank goodness you've come. He's being awful. He bucked me off twice and now I'm afraid to get back on him."

"Have you tried lunging him?" I asked her.

"Yes, he's good on the lunge. He jumped it the first time."

I took hold of his bridle, "What's up with you, you horrible pony?" I stuck my face close to his nose and growled at him. "Would you like *me* to ride him, Ellan? I've had a lot of experience staying on a bucking pony since I've had Jazz!"

It was true. Jazz, for all his faults, had given me tons of confidence. I looked at Rikki. He was so pretty, and at only thirteen two, he seemed small by comparison. This only goes to show that you should never underestimate ponies, however cute they look! I stepped lightly on to him and asked him to walk forward. From the beginning he felt different. His spine stiffened and his ears went back.

"Come on, Rikki," I said sternly, "walk on."

We walked and trotted unhappily around the field, and then I sent him in to the new jump. It was low and bushy but very wide. As we got close he started to back off, I used my stick hard behind the saddle and he leapt forward in surprise. I felt him stiffen even more as he gamely jumped the brush. I was really pleased with myself; I'd gotten him over it when Ellan couldn't!

My pleasure was short-lived. Rikki put his head firmly between his knees and bucked and bucked for all he was worth. For just a few seconds I remained perched on Ellan's horrible, flat saddle, but then I lost my grip and went sailing merrily through the air. Thud! I landed on my back and stared up at the canopy of leaves above my head. My pride was severely damaged. Hopefully, I checked my limbs; a broken bone would at least give my fall some credibility! Everything felt boringly normal so I sat up and watched as Ellan caught her pony.

"That's *exactly* what he did to me," she said gleefully, "twice!"

The saddle had slipped so she undid the girth to straighten it and I noticed Rikki flinch.

"Hang on a minute, Ellan, take the saddle right off. I think he's in pain."

We inspected his back closely but could see nothing except for a small, roughened patch of hair. However, when we looked at the saddle we found that the wooden tree had begun to poke through a hole in the elderly serge lining.

"Well there's our answer," said Ellan. "No wonder he bucked us off. I don't blame him with that sticking in his back! Poor Rikki."

"We'd better take him in and go and work on your mom; you *need* another saddle now. Do you think she's got any of her chocolate cake in the pantry? It's seems like hours since I ate that sandwich."

I sat in Ellan's kitchen and devoured the most delicious chocolate cake in the world, washed down by a glass of milk. Ellan's mom is a terrific cook, unlike her daughter. They both sat at the table and watched me eat.

"*That's* what you have to do if you want to grow bigger," said Mrs. Parry to Ellan, "Eat a bit more. I love to see Paula enjoying her food so much."

This made me feel like an exhibit in a freak show – the Fat Lady – I was beginning to get a complex about my weight.

Between mouthfuls I told Mrs. Parry about Rikki's saddle, but didn't quite have the courage to suggest Ellan needed a new one; that was *her* job. There are boundaries beyond which friendship can't be expected to go!

"I've just remembered," said Mrs. Parry, brightly, "There was a letter for you in the mail, Ellan. It's on the dresser."

"For me? Great, I love getting letters." She bounded excitedly across the room to get it and stood with her slender legs twisted awkwardly around each other while she ripped open the envelope and read the letter.

"Oh wow! I forgot I'd even sent it," she gasped.

"Fantastic! I *don't* believe it!" she shouted at the top of her voice. "Licorice, you're going to be a star!"

Mrs. Parry, Licorice and I exchanged worried glances. Ellan was sometimes a bit dramatic, but this was extreme even by her standards. She danced across the kitchen and waved the letter under her mother's nose.

"Let's see it," Mrs. Parry's voice was calm. She put on her reading glasses and scanned the page.

"Yippee!" she suddenly exploded, making me jump out of my skin and spill my milk.

"Paula," said Mrs. Parry, excitedly, "that film you took of Licorice wrecking my house, well it's been accepted for *Funniest Home Videos*! – We've won $600!"

That called for a celebration – another slice of chocolate cake!

"Yes," I told Adam the next day, "it's going to be shown on that home video show, you know, the one that pays six hundred dollars for each clip. It'll be more if it's voted the best on the show!"

We were creosoting fences on his dad's farm; not the most glamorous job in the world but one I had to put up with if I wanted to be with Adam on a Saturday morning. His face was speckled with little brown spots, so I guessed mine was too.

"She can buy herself a new saddle then," said Adam, looking pleased, "Amazing! All that money for a little messing around! Just think of all the miles of fences I'd have to paint to earn that much cash!"

"A new saddle, and maybe some jodhpurs! That's what was on her shopping list last night. Ellan gets to go on the program too, if she wants, except she can't stand the guy who hosts it!" I told him.

"Would *you* like to go on the show? I could give you a Hollywood tan right now, if you like." Adam grabbed me, and sloshed me with the creosote brush... our work deteriorated after that!

We went in to have some lunch, which had been left in the oven for us by Adam's stepmother. We both smelled strongly of creosote, which was hardly surprising because we were well and truly covered in the stuff.

"You'll live forever," Adam told me cheerfully, reading the label on the can, "Extraordinary preservative qualities guaranteed for wood and other natural materials. Are you a natural material? Unnaturally good looking, I'd say, and now you'll never need a face-lift, either!"

"Adam," I said and then paused. There was something I'd wanted to ask him for a long time. "Adam, do you think I'm fat?"

"Horribly, grossly, revoltingly overweight! That's why I'm going out with you! Now, stop being so silly and have another baked potato!"

# chapter fourteen

Despite school making the days drag by, the Berncarrow
Event came around very quickly. It was an unusually hot
day for September, and Adam and I set off to walk the
course in our T-shirts despite the early hour. We held
hands, laughing all the way to the start. My hilarity ended
when I saw the first jump. It was not just large and solid,
but filled with masses of brightly colored flowers.

"That's it," I said to Adam, "public humiliation number
three! Jazz will take one look at these flowers and buck
me off."

"Don't be so defeatist. He'll just think it's an oddly
colored show jump. I've seen him jump stranger things
than that before."

"*You* don't know how his weird brain works. He'll think
of something horrible to do to me. He always does!" I
replied.

The rest of the course wasn't any more inviting. By the
time I was mounted on Jazz, riding him in, I'd worked
myself into a very negative frame of mind. He picked up
on it and gave two huge bucks that I only just survived. It

didn't improve my mood when I realized that Tony was watching me, leaning against a tree. Mrs. Frost walked over to him and I could feel her stare boring into me.

I returned to the trailer and found Ellan shyly introducing Jason to Freya. I was introduced next and I found myself shaking hands with a tall, pleasant-looking boy with a friendly smile. He had blonde hair and big, white teeth that reminded me a bit of Jazz. He didn't say much but he radiated his good humor and put a protective arm around Ellan.

Adam had much earlier times than I did and had done his show jumping before I'd even started my dressage. I was hot and flustered and Jazz reared twice outside the arena. I was carrying my long whip and, despite disapproving looks from an ignorant but well-meaning bystander, I hit Jazz hard. He went to go up again but this time my voice was enough to stop him. The judge rang her bell and we entered the arena. Jazz seemed surprised by my unaccustomed show of dominance. He trotted meekly up the centerline, and for the following four minutes did exactly what I asked. We rode our best ever test and I was so proud of him it hurt! Grinning from ear to ear I went to find Adam. He was brushing Custar's lean, yellow body while Mr. Bray was busy changing the studs in the gelding's shoes. A horsefly settled on Custar's belly and stung the big horse. I watched in horror as he kicked out blindly, catching Adam's dad with a blow to his face. Mr. Bray stumbled away holding his hand over his mouth.

"Dad! Dad, are you all right? Paula, get the medics quickly."

I did as I was told and soon Mr. Bray was being made comfortable in the ambulance.

"Your dad lost a tooth," a uniformed officer told Adam, "He'll have to go to the emergency room to get checked over. He's lucky it's not worse, if you ask me."

Freya offered to unhitch the car and drive him there. "You'll have to fend for yourselves for a couple of hours. Ellan can help you," she said, as she hurriedly unloaded my tack from the trunk of the car.

We watched them drive away. Ellan, Jason and Adam helped me get ready, and then stood miserably at the ringside and watched me complete a ragged show jumping round. Jazz was behaving, but I was finding it hard to concentrate and I let him get too close to the stile and the pole fell. We tried to cheer ourselves up but, not knowing how badly hurt Mr. Bray really was, we were all unsettled. On top of all that I had the uneasy feeling that there was more to come that day.

"At the moment, Adam's in third place, you're fifth, Paula, because of getting penalties in the show jumping, and that moron, Tony, is second," announced Ellan, returning from a trip to the scoreboard. "Paula, your dressage was beautiful, but not as beautiful as Sally Thorpe's. It's lucky Sally can't jump for beans," she concluded rather unkindly.

I was busy unbraiding Jazz's mane and my mouth was too full of rubber bands to answer.

"Oh, and Adam's almost ready to start," Ellan continued. "I left Jason making himself useful putting grease on

Custar. Why not leave Jazz for ten minutes and come and watch Adam?"

I checked my watch. I had thirty minutes before I was due to ride again, and Jazz was tacked up and ready to go.

"OK, but help me put the trailer ramp up. I don't want Jazz getting loose."

We strained under the weight and struggled with the catches.

"I wish Dad were here. He's got a knack with these bolts."

The ramp was slightly warped and it needed someone strong to fasten it properly.

"Oh, just leave it." It was raised but not fastened. "I'll tie Jazz up short and hope he doesn't pull back on the rope."

We ran down to the start, just in time to see Adam fly over the first fence. Jason was watching, his mouth half open with undisguised admiration.

"Wow, he's going fast!" he exclaimed.

My heart was in my mouth as I watched Adam racing across the field, clearing the jumps effortlessly. It was far more terrifying watching Adam than doing it myself. He went through the water, disappeared into the woods and didn't come out for what seemed like hours but could only have been minutes. I bit my nails until he appeared again and galloped strongly up the hill to the finish. A wave of pride and affection swept over me; I could hardly believe that the good-looking guy who'd just done a perfect clear round was my boyfriend!

"That was a clear round for Adam Bray," the loud speaker was muffled and crackly, "and next to go should be Tony Frost. Would you come to the start please, Tony."

I hurried away back to the trailer. I wanted to avoid meeting Tony if at all possible.

"Loose horse," someone shouted.

Several people were vainly trying to catch a short tailed bay horse that was careering excitedly around the horse trailers, stirrups, reins and lead rope flapping.

*Looks a little like Jazz*, I thought to myself, except for the tail. Then the horse trotted over to me.

"Oh, no!" I shouted, "It *is* Jazz."

He was blowing and snorting with excitement. A small crowd of people were standing around my trailer and I noticed Peter Edmund kneeling on the ground, crouched over somebody.

"Get the ambulance," someone shouted, "Hurry, someone get help!"

A man came toward me and ushered me aside.

"Don't look, honey. Come this way."

"But that's *my* trailer. What happened?" I asked him.

"I'm sorry, hon. I'm afraid your brother's had an accident, but don't worry, your mom's with him," he sounded embarrassed and he didn't meet my gaze.

I was confused. He couldn't mean Adam or Jason. I'd just left them, and as far as I knew Mom was at home looking after Luke.

To my relief, the others arrived at the same time as the ambulance.

"You group are keeping us busy today," said the officer who'd treated Mr. Bray.

"Stand aside, please," said another.

"What's going on, Paula?" asked Adam.

"I don't know, I think some kid's had an accident behind my trailer. Apparently his mom's with him and Peter's there too," I answered, mystified. "Hold Jazz, Jason, I want a closer look,"

I handed him the reins but as I approached the ambulance I was sent back by a worried looking official.

"Keep back, there's nothing you can do," he told me.

"Paula," said Jason, "are your reins meant to be like this?" he pointed to the buckles.

"Like what?" I asked having a closer look. "Oh! No, they're not."

All but one or two of the stitches had been sliced through. Adam checked my girth.

"It looks as though someone doesn't want you to ride. This has been cut, too. Quick, we can change all Jazz's tack for Custar's and get you down to the start. There's still time. Whatever happened here, we'll be better off out of the way for a while."

"They haven't hurt Jazz, have they?" I felt weak and very anxious. Memories of Bella flooded into my mind. Adam ran his hand over Jazz's body and down his legs.

"Nothing, except for chopping his tail off short, and that's only cosmetic." Adam turned to me and whispered, "Paula, you *can't* let this intimidate you. You *must* ride, if only to spite whoever did it."

Between them, Adam and Jason stripped Jazz and re-
placed his tack with Custar's. Ellan strapped me into my
protective vest and legged me into the saddle. It felt unfamiliar and the reins were damp from Custar's sweat.

"You'll be all right," Adam reassured me, "That's my
lucky saddle!"

"You mean it's your only saddle," I retorted.

"Well, that's lucky, isn't it? Now get a move on... and
try to enjoy yourself!"

"Number 76, last call for number 76," droned the loud-
speaker.

"I wish you'd wake up, number 76, I've been calling
you for quite a while," said the starter grumpily.

I was on the course before I knew what was happening.
The fearful flower fence, now tattered and diminished,
flashed beneath us and we galloped to the next, a set of
steps. We climbed them effortlessly and Jazz launched
himself off the top and we headed on down a very steep
hillside. I had planned to trot here, but Jazz had other
ideas. We fought, he won, I shut my eyes and we were at
the bottom, stumbling, tripping, and pitching forward. He
found his feet and I stuck like glue to the strange saddle as
we sped on.

"Listen to me next time," I shouted at him, but I knew
he wouldn't. He was enjoying himself too much. He
skipped through the water and made nothing of the coffin.
I was aware that I was grinning foolishly and I let out a
yell of joy as I settled into the rhythm of his powerful
stride and let the fences come to us. The jumps no longer

seemed big from the back of my lion-hearted horse. He over-jumped the bank, but we stayed upright and galloped up the final hill, the finish in sight and the wind roaring in my ears. Over the rails and we'd done it. Jazz, still full of running, had jumped eighteen difficult fences amazingly fast and brought me home safely. Tears of relief flooded down my face. I leaned forward and urged him through the finish, patting his neck with every stride.

"I love you, I love you," I sobbed as his gallop slowed to a canter, then to a trot. His sides were heaving and sweat ran down his cheeks in little rivulets. I slithered down, my legs shaking. I found some mints in my pocket and he wolfed them all down, and then pushed me with his nose, demanding more. Ellan ran across to me and took over.

"Was he good?" she asked, running up his stirrups and loosening his girth.

"Great, wonderful, fantastic! He was *such* a star," I sniffed.

"Then stop crying! Ooh look, the police are here now."

We watched as two police cars came bumping across the field, just as the ambulance left. Now an even larger crowd had gathered around my trailer. Freya was there and Mr. Bray, who didn't look too much the worse for his accident. Freya was talking to Peter.

"What was he doing by my trailer in the first place?" she asked him, "and where's Paula?"

"Here I am," I called, "Jazz was great! He jumped everything clear, and he..." I trailed off, aware of the ashen faces all around me. "What's the matter?" Fear gripped me, my voice came out as a whisper. "Please, will someone tell me what's happened?"

"It's Tony," said Peter gently, "It seems that he was standing behind the trailer when Jazz broke free. The ramp crushed him."

An awful picture entered my head of the ramp crashing down on Tony with Jazz's crippling weight on top.

"Is he... is he dead?" I whispered.

"No, but they think his back may be broken. I saw it happen. I heard about your Dad, Adam, and I was coming over to give you a hand. I saw Tony putting the ramp up. I wondered what he was doing, and the next second Jazz burst out of the trailer backwards, right on top of Tony, poor guy," Peter sighed.

"Poor guy!" Ellan was indignant as she held out Jazz's reins for everyone to see, "look what he'd been doing in there – it would have been Paula's back that was broken if Jason hadn't noticed that her tack had been tampered with."

"I think we should tell the police about this," said Peter, "Bullying at school is one thing but this is completely different."

"And there's Bella," I said, quietly to Freya, "if Tony could take a knife to Jazz's tack knowing how dangerous that would be for me, then I wouldn't put anything past him."

"Let's just leave all the supposing to the police, okay?" said Freya kindly.

# chapter fifteen

"So Tony ended up in the same hospital as Julie," I said to Freya as we drove home that afternoon. "She will be excited! They can discuss traction together! How romantic! I'll never understand what she sees in him."

"Poor girl," said Freya, with feeling, "you can't always *help* who you fall in love with."

"Urggh," I said.

"What's up, are you feeling sick?" she slowed the car.

"Yes," I said, "I was just thinking how close *I* came to being in the next bed to Tony!"

That evening a policeman and a policewoman came over to the house to ask me some questions. They wanted to know about all the dealings I'd ever had with Tony and his mother. I told them everything, including my suspicions that Tony had thrown the stone that caused Julie's accident, but I don't think they believed this as they said the horse in front of her could have kicked it out.

"You horsy girls," said the detective kindly, "you're always having accidents."

"We've been in touch with the hospital," said Dad, "Tony's got a bad concussion and they're keeping him in overnight, but thankfully they don't think his back is too badly injured."

"Tony admitted to damaging your tack," the Policeman told us, "He says he's sorry. He doesn't know what came over him."

"It's since his father left," said the detective, with more sympathy in her voice than Tony deserved, "He only has his mom now."

I yawned. I couldn't stop myself.

"You're tired," said the officer. "We'll get out of your way now and send a man over in the morning to take photos of your horse's tail. We need to keep your reins and your girth, too. I don't think this will come to court, but if it does we have to be prepared."

"They're not much good to me as they are," I said.

"Right!" he smiled and snapped his book shut. "How did you make out today? I take it from all these sabotage attempts that you must be pretty good!"

"We won," I said simply.

I'd worked so hard to be able to say those two words, but the events of the day had stolen all the glory from them. Tony had succeeded in spoiling it for me; maybe not in the way he'd expected, but no matter how much I hated Tony I couldn't enjoy his plight.

"Jazz had the fastest cross-country time and we won," I repeated, my voice was little more than a whisper. Then, to my embarrassment, I burst into tears.

I went out early the next morning. Jazz was hanging over the paddock gate waiting for breakfast; Bella looked over her stable door and banged it impatiently with her foot. The weather was still mild, but Jazz wore a snug, waterproof rug and a hood; I wouldn't start to bring him in at night until the colder weather. I fed them both and watched as they started to munch appreciatively. I noticed that Jazz had a scratch on his soft muzzle.

"What *have* you been up to?" I asked him, "Playing with the barbed wire again?"

I made a mental note to plead with Dad for post and rail fences, and then I grabbed the purple spray, which was the horsy *cure-all* for wounds. I had to sneak up on Jazz to administer it, as he hates the hissing noise and the cold of the spray.

He ran away from me, snorting his disapproval, but at least some of the spray had reached its target. "Don't be appreciative, then," I said to him.

When they had both finished I turned Bella into the paddock with Jazz and went for my own breakfast.

I had several callers that morning. After breakfast, two policemen arrived. One had a camera to photograph Jazz's tail, and the other one asked to speak to Dad alone.

"Will you show me this dock tailed nag of yours?" the policeman asked, jokingly, with his camera slung around his neck, "I don't know one end of a horse from the other!"

"The horses have wandered down to the lower field," I told him, "I'll show you the way."

"Paula," Mom called from the kitchen window, "phone call for you."

"I'll make my own way down," said the policeman, who was somewhat plump – his uniform was stretched tightly over his stomach.

"What's he look like, this horse of yours? How will I know which one to photograph?"

"He's the bay gelding in the New Zealand," I told him, but the Policeman just stared at me blankly. "He's brown with four black legs, one head, half a tail and wearing a waterproof rug!"

"That's more like it," said the fat one and he waddled off in the direction of the field.

I dashed in and picked up the phone. I was expecting it to be Ellan so I was very surprised when Captain Hewit's voice boomed in my ear.

"Hello, Paula, thought I'd phone and congratulate you on your performance yesterday. Well done! You seem to have gotten that brazen horse of yours under control at last!" he guffawed loudly.

"Thank you very much. Jazz was good for once," I replied, a little taken aback by the Captain's show of good humor – it wasn't even lunchtime yet!

"Awful thing that happened to young Frost. It's his mother I feel sorry for."

"Well I don't," I said angrily.

"No, I don't suppose you do. Anyway, I really called to say that there will be a place on the junior Pony Club team for you next season, if you're interested."

I should say I was interested! After the Captain hung up I sat staring into space for quite a while, savoring the news.

Then Adam arrived, hot and puffing gently from having biked ten miles.

"There's a beautiful old motorcycle in the road," he told me, " It's leaned against your hedge. Seems to have been there all night, judging by the dew on it."

"You're not a bike fanatic are you?" I asked him.

"I like *all* machines... comes from being a farmer's boy," he assured me.

We wandered down the sloping paddock to find the fat policeman. As we passed through the second gate we met him coming the other way.

"Don't go down there, kids!" he panted, "It's not a pretty sight! Not a pretty sight at all," he muttered to himself.

My heart leaped violently into my mouth,

"The horses, what's happened to the horses?" I was almost crying with fear.

"It's all right, dear, your *horses* are fine, but there's a guy down by the hedge who doesn't look too good."

For the next few hours our house buzzed with various policemen, a doctor and two detectives. They eventually removed our mystery guest – Adam and I watched from the kitchen window as a body, unconscious, bruised and battered, was placed in an ambulance.

We answered numerous questions until our heads spun.

Finally Dad came into the kitchen, slumped down in a chair and said, "They're gone, though I'd bet anything they'll be back soon, this time with the Press."

"Do they know who he is, Mr. Wilkie?" Adam asked.

"No, but one of the detectives is fairly sure he knows him. It's someone they've been observing for quite some time."

"How did he get so badly hurt?" Mom asked.

It was one of the questions we'd been mulling over all day. The other question was, *what was the man doing in our field in the first place*? Freya thought he may have come off his bike and been thrown into the paddock, but Adam said that the bike wasn't damaged.

Adam and I thought he'd been chased and shot by a gang of desperate gangsters... we didn't really, but there just didn't seem to be a sensible answer.

"He received a blow to the head," said Dad.

"There you are," I turned to Adam, "bludgeoned by a rival gang!" It was so awful that I needed to try and make light of it.

"It's not funny, Paula," said Mom sharply.

"It seems…" Dad said, very slowly, "… it *seems* as though Jazz probably kicked him in the head."

The world started to spin. I gripped the arms of my chair in the hope that it would stop me from fainting.

"This man," Dad went on, "is crazy. He's been prosecuted before for hurting horses, and when they found him this morning he had a knife and some rope with him. The detectives think that he probably came back for another go at Bella... but he met up with Jazz instead. We may not know for quite some time. Jazz won't tell us and our visitor certainly can't at the moment."

"Will Jazz have to be put down?" my lip was trembling, I knew how the law dealt with vicious dogs; maybe Jazz would be viewed in the same light.

"Don't worry about that, Paula," said Mom, "if someone's *wicked* enough and *stupid* enough to go wielding a knife around a horse then they deserve all they get. Jazz is more likely to be awarded a medal for bravery!"

Later, when we were all sick of talking about it, Adam took my hand and led me down the paddock to visit Jazz and Bella.

"I remember when you had that crashing fall on Bella at the Area Trials," Adam told me as we wandered across the short, cropped turf.

"How can you remember that? I didn't know who you were then," I said.

"You may not have noticed *me*, but I noticed you a long time ago!"

Bella wandered over and inspected our pockets, but Jazz stayed aloof at the far end of the field. The police had been a great disappointment to him, with pockets full of paper, not Polos.

"Hello, old girl," Adam smoothed Bella's tousled mane and ran his hand down her dusty neck. "Wow, Paula, is that what he did to her?" he said pointing to the scars.

"Yes, I'm glad it's not a secret any more. It felt weird not telling you."

"Phew! Poor old girl. Still, she looks healthy enough, apart from that. Nice and plump."

I stared hard at her. Adam was right, she was somewhat round, but it wasn't the typical fatness that you normally associate with a grass belly. This was heavier and sort of squared off toward the back. A little feeling of excitement ignited like a sparkler deep inside me. I put my hand on the mare's flank and for the first time since the attack she nuzzled me affectionately. With the strange communication that is sometimes possible between animals and people I knew then, without ever doubting it, that she was still carrying her foal.

We sat down on the grass and watched the horses grazing. I felt happier and safer than I had for months.

"So the Captain wants you on the team – that means we might get to go to the Championships together next year," mused Adam.

"Yes, it's great, isn't it?" Next year now felt secure and full of the promise of many wonderful and exciting things. I sighed a deep and very contented sigh and cuddled up more closely to Adam.

"Was the Captain his usual charming self?" Adam asked.

"He was actually nice to me. It's funny, though. He re-ferred to Jazz as my *Brazen Horse* – I thought that was odd. He doesn't know about the model, does he?"

Adam started chuckling to himself.

"What's so funny?" I don't like being teased.

"It's the word brazen. It can mean two things; either something that's made out of brass, maybe shiny and polished..."

"Or?" I asked. I had the feeling I wasn't going to like the *or*.

"Or," said Adam, very slowly, "it *can* mean... overconfident, shameless, disrespectful, arrogant, nervy... shall I go on?"

I hated to admit it, but that sounded *exactly* like Jazz!